Welcome to the United States

A Guide for New Immigrants

U.S. Citizenship
and Immigration
Services

U.S. GOVERNMENT OFFICIAL EDITION NOTICE

3 1257 01702 8027

Use of ISBN Prefix

This is the Official U.S. Government edition of this publication and is herein identified to certify its authenticity. Use of the 0-16 ISBN prefix is for U.S. Government Printing Office Official Editions only. The Superintendent of Documents of the U.S. Government Printing Office requests that any reprinted edition clearly be labeled as a copy of the authentic work with a new ISBN.

The information presented in *Welcome to the United States: A Guide for New Immigrants* is considered public information and may be distributed or copied without alteration unless otherwise specified. The citation should be:

U.S. Department of Homeland Security, U.S. Citizenship and Immigration Services, Office of Citizenship, *Welcome to the United States: A Guide for New Immigrants*, Washington, DC, 2005.

USCIS has purchased the right to use many of the images in *Welcome to the United States: A Guide for New Immigrants*. USCIS is licensed to use these images on a non-exclusive and non-transferable basis. All other rights to the image, including without limitation and copyright, are retained by the owner of the images. These images are not in the public domain and may not be used except as they appear as part of this guide.

This guide contains information on a variety of topics that are not within the jurisdiction of DHS/USCIS. If you have a question about a non DHS/USCIS issue, please refer directly to the responsible agency or organization for the most current information. This information is correct at the time of printing; however, it may change in the future.

For sale by the Superintendent of Documents, U.S. Government Printing Office
Internet: bookstore.gpo.gov   Phone: toll free (866) 512-1800;   DC area (202) 512-1800
Fax: (202) 512-2250 Mail: Stop SSOP, Washington, DC 20402-0001

ISBN 13: 978-0-16-072393-3
ISBN 10: 0-16-072393-0

Welcome to the United States
A Guide for New Immigrants

Congratulations on becoming a permanent resident of the United States of America. On behalf of the President of the United States and the American people, we welcome you and wish you every success in the United States.

The United States has a long history of welcoming immigrants from all parts of the world. America values the contributions of immigrants, who continue to enrich this country and preserve its legacy as a land of freedom and opportunity.

As a permanent resident of the United States, you have made a decision to call this country your home. As you work to achieve your goals, take some time to get to know this country, its history, and its people. It is now both your right and your responsibility to shape the future of this country and ensure its continued success.

Exciting opportunities await you as you begin your life as a resident of this great country. Welcome to the United States!

U.S. Citizenship and Immigration Services

GETTING SETTLED IN THE UNITED STATES

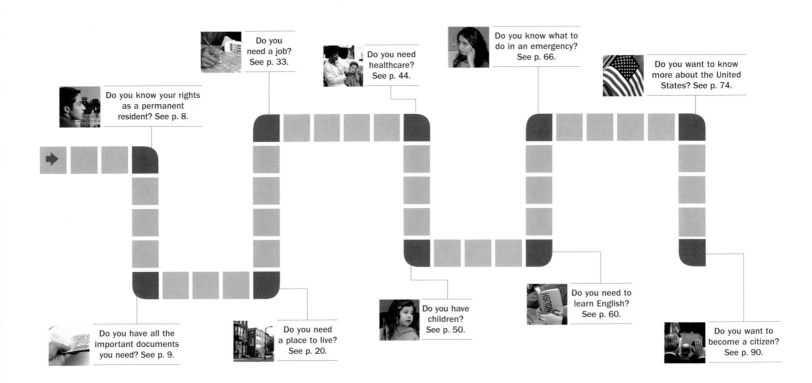

Do you need a job? See p. 33.

Do you need healthcare? See p. 44.

Do you know what to do in an emergency? See p. 66.

Do you want to know more about the United States? See p. 74.

Do you know your rights as a permanent resident? See p. 8.

Do you have all the important documents you need? See p. 9.

Do you need a place to live? See p. 20.

Do you have children? See p. 50.

Do you need to learn English? See p. 60.

Do you want to become a citizen? See p. 90.

TABLE OF CONTENTS

FEDERAL DEPARTMENTS AND AGENCIES

If you are not sure which department to call about a question, start by calling 1-800-FED-INFO (or 1-800-333-4636) to ask where to call. People who have difficulty hearing can call 1-800-326-2996. You can also visit http://www.FirstGov.gov for general information about federal departments and agencies.

Department of Education (ED)
U.S. Department of Education
400 Maryland Avenue SW
Washington, DC 20202

Phone: 1-800-872-5327
For hearing impaired: 1-800-437-0833
http://www.ed.gov

Equal Employment Opportunity Commission (EEOC)
U. S. Equal Employment Opportunity Commission
1801 L Street NW
Washington, DC 20507
Phone: 1-800-669-4000
For hearing impaired: 1-800-669-6820
http://www.eeoc.gov

Department of Health and Human Services (HHS)
U.S. Department of Health and Human Services
200 Independence Avenue SW
Washington, DC 20201
Phone: 1-877-696-6775
http://www.hhs.gov

Department of Homeland Security (DHS)
U.S. Department of Homeland Security
Washington, DC 20528
http://www.dhs.gov

U. S. Citizenship and Immigration Services (USCIS)
Phone: 1-800-375-5283
For hearing impaired: 1-800-767-1833
http://www.uscis.gov

U.S. Customs and Border Protection (CBP)
Phone: 1-202-354-1000
http://www.cbp.gov

U. S. Immigration and Customs Enforcement (ICE)
http://www.ice.gov

Department of Housing and Urban Development (HUD)

U.S. Department of Housing and Urban Development
451 7th Street SW
Washington, DC 20410
Phone: 1-202-708-1112
For hearing impaired: 1-202-708-1455
http://www.hud.gov

Department of Justice (DOJ)

U.S. Department of Justice
950 Pennsylvania Avenue NW
Washington, DC 20530-0001
Phone: 1-202-514-2000
http://www.usdoj.gov

Internal Revenue Service (IRS)

Phone: 1-800-829-1040
For hearing impaired: 1-800-829-4059
http://www.irs.gov

Selective Service System (SSS)

Registration Information Office
PO Box 94638
Palatine, IL 60094-4638
Phone: 1-847-688-6888
For hearing impaired: 1-847-688-2567
http://www.sss.gov

Social Security Administration (SSA)

Office of Public Inquiries
6401 Security Boulevard
Baltimore, MD 21235
Phone: 1-800-772-1213
For hearing impaired: 1-800-325-0778
http://www.socialsecurity.gov

Department of State (DOS)

U.S. Department of State
2201 C Street NW
Washington, DC 20520
Phone: 1-202-647-4000
http://www.state.gov

TO GET MORE INFORMATION FROM USCIS:

Visit our website at http://www.uscis.gov.

Call our National Customer Service Center:
1-800-375-5283 or 1-800-767-1833 (hearing impaired).

To get USCIS forms, call 1-800-870-3676 or look on
the USCIS website.

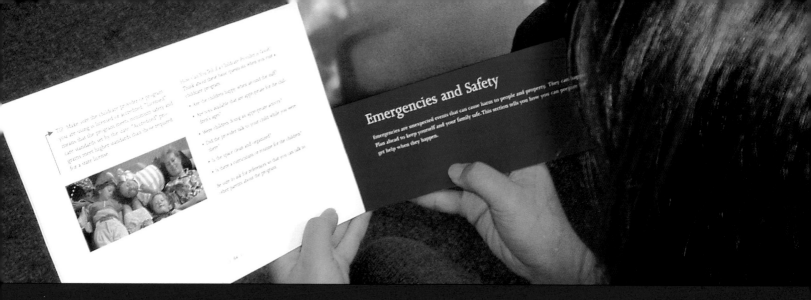

About This Guide

Adjusting to your new life in the United States of America will take time. This guide contains basic information that will help you settle in the United States and find what you and your family need for everyday life. It also summarizes important information about your legal status and about agencies and organizations that provide documents or essential services you may need.

As a permanent resident, you should begin to learn about this country, its people, and its system of government. Use this guide to find out about your rights and responsibilities as a new immigrant, to understand how our federal, state, and local governments work, and to learn how important historical events have shaped the United States. This guide also explains the importance of getting involved in your own community and offers suggestions to help you do so.

This guide provides a general summary of rights, responsibilities, and procedures related to permanent residents. To get more specific and detailed information, you should consult the laws, regulations, forms, and guidance of U.S. Citizenship and Immigration Services (USCIS). You should always consult these more detailed resources for your specific immigration question or case. Most of the information you need can be found on the USCIS website at http://www.uscis.gov. You can obtain USCIS forms by calling 1-800-870-3676 and you can get more information by calling the USCIS National Customer Service Center at 1-800-375-5283 or 1-800-767-1833 (for hearing impaired).

Where to Get Help

This guide will help you get started, but it cannot answer all the questions you have about life in the United States. To find additional information, you may wish to contact a state, county, or city government office to learn about services you need or consult with a local organization that helps new immigrants settle into life here. You can find these offices and organizations by using the free resources described below.

The Public Library
Public libraries in the United States are free and open to everyone. Libraries are located in almost every community. The library staff can help you find information on almost any topic and can give you a library card that allows you to borrow items, such as books and videotapes, free of charge. Most libraries also have local newspapers for you to read and computers that you can use to search the Internet. Ask the library staff to show you how to use the computer to search the Internet.

Some libraries give free classes on how to search the Internet. Some libraries also provide English language tutoring or classes and other programs for children and adults.

Your Local Phone Book

Your local "phone book" (telephone directory) contains phone numbers and important information about federal, state, and local community services. The phone book has emergency information, local maps, and information about how to get phone service. The white pages list phone numbers of individual people; the yellow pages have phone numbers and addresses for businesses and organizations; and the blue pages show local, state, and federal government office phone numbers and addresses. You can also dial 411 on your phone to get a specific phone number anywhere in the United States. Your community or city also may have a separate book with the yellow pages listings or its own community phone book.

The Internet

The Internet can link you to many sources of information, including the websites of federal, state, and local government agencies. Most government websites end with ".gov". If you don't have a computer at home, you can use one in your public library or at an "Internet café," which is a business that charges a fee for using a computer with Internet service. You can use the Internet to search for jobs, find housing, learn about schools for your children, and locate community organizations and resources to help you. You also can discover interesting information on the Internet about life in America, United States history and government, and your local community.

> TIP: As an immigrant you should be aware that dishonest people have made websites that look like government websites to confuse you and take advantage of you. Remember that http://www.uscis.gov is the official website of U.S. Citizenship and Immigration Services.

Community- and Faith-Based Organizations That Assist Immigrants

There are organizations in many communities that provide free or very low-cost assistance to immigrants. These organizations can help you learn about your community and the services available to you as an immigrant. You can look for these organizations by searching on the Internet, looking in your local phone book, asking at the public library, and asking your local government social service agency.

Getting Involved in Your Community

Getting involved in your community will help you feel at home here. Your community is also a good source of information. Here are some ways to get involved:

• Introduce yourself to and get to know your neighbors.

• Talk with or visit community organizations that help immigrants get settled in the U.S.

• Join groups at your place of worship.

• Join your neighborhood association. This is a group of people in the neighborhood who meet to work together on things affecting the neighborhood.

• Volunteer at a community organization, school, or place of worship.

• Enroll in an English language class.

You can find more ideas about getting involved on the Department of Housing and Urban Development's website at http://www.hud.gov. Look in the "Communities" section for information about communities and suggestions for getting involved.

TO GET MORE INFORMATION FROM USCIS:

 Visit our website at http://www.uscis.gov.

 Call our National Customer Service Center:
1-800-375-5283 or 1-800-767-1833 (hearing impaired).

 To get USCIS forms, call 1-800-870-3676
or look on the USCIS website.

Your Rights and Responsibilities as a Permanent Resident

As a permanent resident, you are expected to respect and be loyal to the United States and to obey our country's laws. Being a permanent resident also means that you have new rights and responsibilities.

Being a permanent resident is a "privilege" and not a "right." The U.S. government can take away your permanent resident status under certain conditions. You must maintain your permanent resident status if you want to live and work in the United States and become a U.S. citizen one day. In this section, you will learn what it means to be a permanent resident and how you can maintain your permanent resident status.

Your Rights and Responsibilities

What you do now as a permanent resident can affect your ability to become a U.S. citizen later. The process of becoming a U.S. citizen is called "naturalization."

As a permanent resident, you have the right to:

- Live and work permanently anywhere in the U.S.

- Apply to become a U.S. citizen once you are eligible.

- Request a visa for your husband or wife and unmarried children to live in the U.S.

- Get Social Security, Supplemental Security Income, and Medicare benefits, if you are eligible.

- Own property in the U.S.

- Apply for a driver's license in your state or territory.

- Leave and return to the U.S. under certain conditions.

- Attend public school and college.

- Join certain branches of the U.S. Armed Forces.

- Purchase or own a firearm, as long as there are no state or local restrictions saying you can't.

As a permanent resident, it is your responsibility to:

- Obey all federal, state, and local laws.

- Pay federal, state, and local income taxes.

- Register with the Selective Service (U.S. Armed Forces), if you are a male between ages 18 and 26. See page 11 for instructions.

- Maintain your immigration status.

- Carry proof of your permanent resident status at all times.

- Give your new address in writing to the Department of Homeland Security (DHS) within 10 days of each time you move. See page 12 for instructions.

Permanent residents are issued a valid Permanent Resident Card (Form I-551) as proof of their legal status in the United States. Some people call this a "Green Card." If you are a permanent resident who is 18 years or older, you must carry proof of your immigration status. You must show it to an immigration officer if asked for it. Your card is valid for 10 years and must be renewed before it expires. You should file Form I-90 to replace or renew your Permanent Resident Card. You can get this form at http://www.uscis.gov or by calling the USCIS Forms Line. There is a fee to file Form I-90.

Your Permanent Resident Card shows that you are allowed to live and work in the United States. You also can use your Permanent Resident Card to re-enter the United States. If you are outside the U.S. for more than 12 months, you will need to show additional documentation to re-enter the U.S. as a permanent resident. See page 10 for more information on the documents required to re-enter the U.S. if you are out of the country for more than 12 months.

OTHER IMPORTANT DOCUMENTS

Keep important documents you brought from your home country in a safe place. These documents include your passport, birth certificate, marriage certificate, divorce certificate, diplomas showing that you have graduated from high school or college, and certificates that show you have special training or skills.

Maintaining Your Permanent Resident Status

There are some things you must do to maintain your permanent resident status. These are also important to remember if you plan to apply for U.S. citizenship in the future.

- Don't leave the United States for an extended period of time or move to another country to live there permanently.

- File federal and state income tax returns.

- Register with the Selective Service, if you are a male between the ages of 18 and 26.

- Give your new address to DHS.

Keep Your Immigration Status

Permanent residents who leave the United States for extended periods, or who cannot show their intent to live permanently in the U.S., may lose their permanent resident status. If you think you will be out of the U.S. for more than 12 months, you should apply for a re-entry permit <u>before</u> leaving the country. You should file Form I-131, Application for a Travel Document. A re-entry permit is valid for up to 2 years and shows that you are returning from a temporary visit abroad. You may show the re-entry permit at a port of entry.

You can get this form at http://www.uscis.gov or by calling the USCIS Forms Line. You must pay a fee to file Form I-131.

If you are not able to return to the U.S. before your re-entry permit expires or you did not apply for a re-entry permit before leaving the U.S. and have been outside the U.S. for more than 12 months, you may be able to get a special immigrant Returning Resident (SB-1) visa overseas from the Department of State. There are special requirements for this visa. Visit http://www.state.gov or your nearest Department of State Consular Office overseas for more information.

File Tax Returns

As a permanent resident, you must file income tax returns and report your income to the Internal Revenue Service (IRS) and your state, city, or local tax department, if required. If you do not file income tax returns while living outside of the U.S. for any length of time, or if you say that you are a "non-immigrant" on your tax returns, the U.S. government may decide that you have given up your permanent resident status.

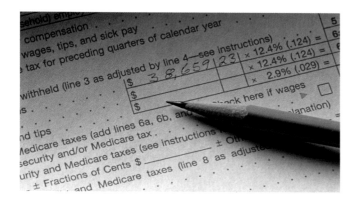

Register With the Selective Service

If you are a man and you are 18 to 26 years old, you must register with the Selective Service. When you register, you tell the government that you are available to serve in the U.S. Armed Forces. The United States does not have a military draft now. Permanent residents and citizens do not have

to serve in the Armed Forces unless they want to.

You can register at a United States post office or on the Internet. To register for Selective Service on the Internet, visit the Selective Service website: http://www.sss.gov. To speak with someone from the Selective Service, call 1-847-688-6888. This is not a free call.

You can also find information on the USCIS website http://www.uscis.gov.

Give Your New Address to DHS

Every time you move, you need to tell DHS your new address. You must file Form AR-11, Alien's Change of Address Card. You must file this form within 10 days of your move. There is no fee to file this form.

Send Form AR-11 to:
Department of Homeland Security
U.S. Citizenship and Immigration Services
Change of Address
P.O. Box 7134
London, KY 40742-7134

For more information, call USCIS at 1-800-375-5283 or visit http://www.uscis.gov/graphics/formsfee/forms/ar-11.htm.

If You Are a Conditional Resident

You may be in the U.S. as a conditional resident (CR). You are a CR if you were married for less than 2 years to your U.S. citizen or permanent resident spouse on the day your permanent resident status was granted. If you have children, they also may be CRs. Some immigrant investors are also conditional residents.

A CR has the same rights and responsibilities as a permanent resident. Conditional residents must file either Form I-751, Petition to Remove the Conditions on Residence, or Form I-829, Petition by Entrepreneur to Remove Conditions, within 2 years of the date they were granted conditional permanent resident status. This date is usually the expiration date of your Permanent Resident Card. You should file these forms within 90 days of the 2-year anniversary of when you got your conditional resident status. If you do not do this, you can lose your immigration status.

Filing Form I-751 With Your Husband or Wife
If you are a CR and you are married, then you and your spouse must file Form I-751 together so that you can remove the conditions on your permanent resident status.

Sometimes, you do not have to file Form I-751 with your husband or wife. If you are no longer married to your spouse, or if your spouse has abused you, you can file Form I-751 by yourself. If you are not applying with your spouse, you can file Form I-751 at any time after you are a CR.

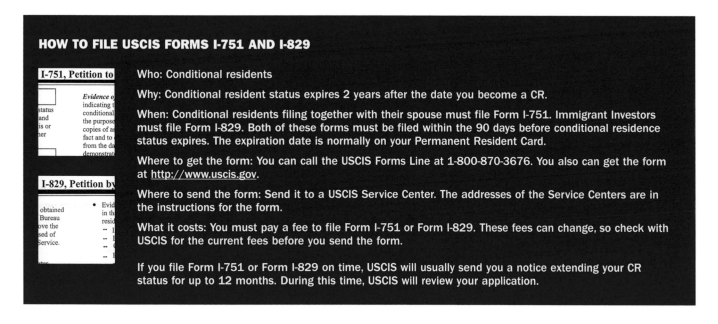

HOW TO FILE USCIS FORMS I-751 AND I-829

Who: Conditional residents

Why: Conditional resident status expires 2 years after the date you become a CR.

When: Conditional residents filing together with their spouse must file Form I-751. Immigrant Investors must file Form I-829. Both of these forms must be filed within the 90 days before conditional residence status expires. The expiration date is normally on your Permanent Resident Card.

Where to get the form: You can call the USCIS Forms Line at 1-800-870-3676. You also can get the form at http://www.uscis.gov.

Where to send the form: Send it to a USCIS Service Center. The addresses of the Service Centers are in the instructions for the form.

What it costs: You must pay a fee to file Form I-751 or Form I-829. These fees can change, so check with USCIS for the current fees before you send the form.

If you file Form I-751 or Form I-829 on time, USCIS will usually send you a notice extending your CR status for up to 12 months. During this time, USCIS will review your application.

TIP: Keep copies of all forms you send to USCIS and other government offices. When sending documents, do not send originals. Send copies. Sometimes forms get lost. Keeping copies can help avoid problems.

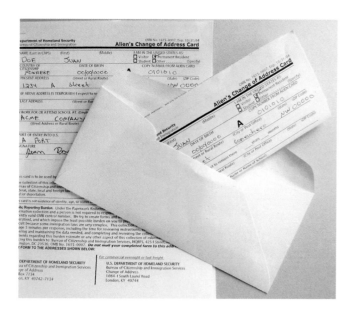

Finding Legal Assistance

If you need help with an immigration issue, you can use the services of a licensed and competent immigration lawyer. You can check with your local bar association for help finding a qualified lawyer.

If you need legal help on an immigration issue, but do not have enough money to hire a lawyer, there are some low-cost or free assistance options. You can ask for help from:

- **A Recognized Organization.** These are organizations that are recognized by the Board of Immigration Appeals (BIA). For an organization to be "recognized," it must have enough knowledge and experience to provide services to immigrants, and can charge or accept only very small fees for those services. For a list of these BIA-recognized organizations, see http://www.usdoj.gov/eoir/statspub/recognitionaccreditationroster.pdf.

- **An Accredited Representative.** These are people who are connected to BIA "recognized organizations."

These representatives can charge or accept only very small fees for their services. For a list of these BIA-accredited representatives, see http://www.usdoj.gov/eoir/statspub/accreditedreproster.pdf.

- **A Qualified Representative.** These are people who will provide free services. These representatives must know about immigration law and the rules of practice in court. Examples of qualified representatives include law school students and graduates and people with good moral character who have a personal or professional affiliation with you (relative, neighbor, clergy, co-worker, friend).

- **Free Legal Service Providers.** The Office of the Chief Immigration Judge has a list of recognized free legal service providers for people who are in immigration proceedings (see http://www.usdoj.gov/eoir/probono/states.htm). This is a list of attorneys and organizations that may be willing to represent immigrants in proceedings before the Immigration Courts. The attorneys and organizations on this list have agreed to help immigrants *pro bono* (free of charge) only in immigration proceedings, so some of them may not be able to help you with non-court-related matters (that is, visa petitions, naturalization, etc.).

IF YOU ARE A VICTIM OF DOMESTIC ABUSE

If you are a victim of domestic abuse, you can find help through the National Domestic Violence Hotline at 1-800-799-7233 or 1-800-787-3224 (for hearing impaired). Help is available in Spanish and other languages.

The Violence Against Women Act allows abused spouses and children of U.S. citizens and permanent residents to "self-petition," or file their own petition to become a permanent resident. See http://uscis.gov/graphics/howdoi/battered.htm or call the National Domestic Violence Hotline for more information.

- **Pro Bono Program**. Local lists of recognized *pro bono* (free of charge) organizations and their representatives are usually available at each local USCIS office.

Beware of Immigration Consultant Fraud!
Many immigration practitioners are well qualified and honest and can provide good services to immigrants. However, there are some people who take advantage of immigrants.

Before you decide to get help with immigration matters, and before you pay any money, you should do some research so you can make the right decision about what kind of legal help you need. Protect yourself from becoming a victim of immigration fraud.

Here are some things to remember:

- No private organization or person offering help with immigration issues has a special connection with USCIS. Ask questions of people who make promises that sound too good to be true or who claim to have a special relationship with USCIS. Do not trust people who guarantee results or faster processing. If you are not eligible for an immigration benefit, using an immigration lawyer or consultant will not change that.

- Some consultants, travel agencies, real estate offices, and people called "notaries public" offer immigration services. Be sure to ask questions about their qualifications and ask to see copies of their BIA accreditation letter or bar certificate. Some people who say they are qualified to offer legal services are not. These people can make mistakes that cause serious problems for you.

- If you use an immigration consultant or lawyer, get a written contract. The contract should be in English and in your own language, if English is not your native language. The contract should list all services that will be provided to you and how much they cost. Ask for references before you sign the contract.

- Try to avoid paying cash for services. Make sure you get a receipt for your payment. Be sure to keep your original documents.

- Never sign a blank form or application. Make sure you understand what you are signing.

Get help if an immigration consultant has cheated you. Call your state or local district attorney, consumer affairs department, or local police department.

Consequences of Criminal Behavior for Permanent Residents

The United States is a law-abiding society. Permanent residents in the United States must obey all laws. If you are a permanent resident and engage in or are convicted of a crime in the U.S., you could have serious problems. You could be removed from the country, not allowed back into the U.S. if you leave the country, and, in certain circumstances, lose your eligibility for U.S. citizenship. Examples of crimes that may affect your permanent resident status include:

- A crime defined as an "aggravated felony," which includes crimes of violence that are felonies with a 1-year prison term.

- Murder.

- Terrorist activities.

- Rape.

- Sexual assault on a child.

- Trafficking in drugs, firearms, or people.

- A crime of "moral turpitude," which in general is a crime with an intent to steal or defraud; a crime where physical harm is done or threatened; a crime where serious physical harm is caused by reckless behavior; or a crime of sexual misconduct.

There are also serious consequences for you as a permanent resident if you:

- Lie to get immigration benefits for yourself or someone else.

- Say you are a U.S. citizen if you are not.

- Vote in a federal election or in a local election open only to U.S. citizens.

- Are a "habitual drunkard"—someone who is drunk or someone who uses illegal drugs most of the time.

- Are married to more than 1 person at the same time.

- Fail to support your family or to pay child or spousal support as ordered.

- Are arrested for assaulting or harassing a family member, including violating a protection order. This is called domestic violence.

- Lie to get public benefits.

- Fail to file tax returns when required.

- Willfully fail to register for the Selective Service if you are a male between the ages of 18 and 26.

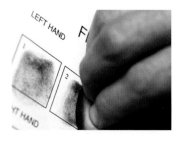

If you have committed or have been convicted of a crime, before you apply for another immigration benefit you should consult with a reputable immigration lawyer or a community-based organization that provides legal service to immigrants. See page 14 for information on how to find legal assistance.

Getting Settled in the United States

This section provides information that can help you adjust to life in the United States. You'll learn about finding housing and a job, getting a Social Security number and a driver's license, taking care of your money, and getting healthcare for you and your family.

Finding a Place to Live

You can choose where you want to live in the United States. Many people stay with friends or family members when they first arrive. After they find jobs, they move into their own housing. Sometimes religious or community organizations also help with temporary housing.

In the United States, most people spend about 25 percent of their income on housing. Here are some of your housing choices:

Renting a Home

Apartments and houses can be rented. You can find these in several ways:

- Look for "Apartment Available" or "For Rent" signs on buildings.

- Look in the newspaper in the section called "Classified Advertisements" or "Classifieds." Find the pages listing "Apartments for Rent" and "Homes for Rent." These will have information about homes, such as where they are located, the number of rooms, and the cost of rent.

- Look in the phone book yellow pages under "Property Management." These are companies that rent homes. These companies may charge you a fee to help you find a home.

- Ask friends and relatives or people at your job if they know of places to rent.

- Check bulletin boards in libraries, grocery stores, and community centers for "For Rent" notices.

- Check for rentals on the Internet. If you don't have a computer at home, you can go to your local public library or an Internet café.

- Call a local real estate agent.

Applying to Rent. People who rent out apartments or homes are called "landlords." A landlord may ask you to fill out a rental application form. This is so the landlord can check to see if you have the money to pay the rent.

The application form may ask for a Social Security number and proof that you are working. You can use your Permanent Resident Card if you do not yet have a Social Security number. You can also show a pay stub from your job to prove you are working. You may also be asked to pay a small application fee.

If you are not yet working, you may need someone to sign the rental agreement with you. This person is called a "co-signer." If you cannot pay the rent, the co-signer will have to pay the rent for you.

Signing a Lease. You sign a rental agreement or "lease" if the landlord agrees to rent to you. When you sign a lease, you agree to pay your rent on time and stay for a specific length of time. Most leases are for 1 year. You can also find housing for shorter periods of time, such as 1 month. You may have to pay more money for a short lease than for a longer one.

When you sign a lease, you agree to keep the home clean and in good shape. You may be charged extra if you damage the place you are renting. The lease may also list the number of people who can live in the home.

A lease is a legal document. You must keep up your part of the agreement. Landlords must also do their part. They must keep the property safe and in good condition.

Paying a Security Deposit. Renters usually pay a security deposit when they move in. This deposit is usually equal to one month's rent. You will get this deposit back if the home is clean and in good condition when you move out. If not, the landlord may keep some or all of your deposit to pay for cleaning or repairs.

Inspect the house or apartment before you move in. Tell the landlord about any problems you find. Talk to your landlord before you move out to find out what you need to fix to get all of your security deposit back.

Paying Other Rental Costs. For some houses or apartments, the rent payment includes the cost of utilities (gas, electricity, heat, water, and trash removal). For other rentals, you must pay separately for these expenses. Ask the landlord if utilities are included when you are looking for housing. If they are, make sure this is in your rental agreement before you sign it. If utilities are not included, you should find out how much they will cost. The cost of some utilities will be more in the summer (for air conditioning) or winter (for heat).

GETTING THINGS FIXED

Landlords must keep the home or apartment you rent safe and in good condition. If you have a problem:

- First, talk to your landlord. Tell him or her what is wrong and that you want it fixed.
- Next, write a letter to your landlord telling him or her what is wrong. Keep a copy for yourself.
- Finally, call your local Housing Office. Most city or local governments have people who inspect houses for problems. Ask the inspector to visit and show him or her all the problems.

If your landlord does not fix the problems, you may be able to make a legal charge against him or her.

Ending a Lease. Ending a rental agreement is called "terminating your lease." Your landlord may agree to terminate your lease early if he or she can find someone else to rent your home. If not, you may have to pay monthly rent until the end of the lease, even if you are not living there. You also may lose your security deposit if you leave before the end of the lease. Give your landlord a written notice that you want to move out. Most landlords require notice at least 30 days before you want to leave.

KNOW YOUR RIGHTS: DISCRIMINATION IN HOUSING IS NOT ALLOWED

Landlords cannot refuse to rent to you because of who you are. It is against the law for landlords to reject you because of:

- your race or color.
- the country you came from.
- your religion.
- your sex.
- a physical disability.
- your family status, such as whether or not you are married.

If you feel you have been refused housing for any of these reasons, you can contact the U.S. Department of Housing and Urban Development (HUD) by phone at 1-800-669-9777. Information is given in English and Spanish.

TIP: If you move, you should tell the U.S. Postal Service so it can forward your mail to your new address. You can change your address online at http://www.usps.com or visit your local post office and request a "Moving Guide." Don't forget to also file Form AR-11 with DHS. See page 12 for instructions.

Buying a Home

For many people owning a home is part of the "American Dream." Owning a home has many benefits and brings many responsibilities.

Real estate agents can help you find a home to buy. Ask friends or co-workers or call a local real estate agency for the name of an agent. Ask for an agent who knows the area where you want to buy your house. You can look in the newspaper "Classifieds" under "Homes for Sale." You can also look for "For Sale" signs in the neighborhoods you like.

Most people need to get a loan to pay for a home; this is called a "mortgage." You can get a mortgage from a

local bank or from a mortgage company. Getting a mortgage means you are borrowing money at a specific rate of interest for a specific period of time.

Interest you pay on your mortgage can be deducted from your federal income tax.

TIP: Beware of lenders charging very high interest rates on mortgages. Some lenders may try to charge you more because you are new to this country. There are laws to protect you from fraud, unnecessary expenses, and discrimination in buying a home. Find out more by visiting the "Homes" section at http://www.hud.gov.

You also need to buy homeowner's insurance to help pay for any possible future damage to your home. Insurance usually covers damage due to bad weather, fire, or robbery. You will also need to pay property taxes on the value of your home.

A real estate agent or real estate lawyer can help you find a mortgage and insurance. He or she can also help you fill out the forms to buy your home. A real estate agent should not charge you a fee to buy a home. But you may have to pay a fee to a real estate lawyer to help you fill out the forms. You will also have to pay fees to get your mortgage and to file legal forms with the state. These fees are called "closing costs." Your real estate agent or mortgage lender must tell you how much these fees will be before you sign the final purchase forms for your home.

MORE INFORMATION ABOUT BUYING OR RENTING A HOME

Visit the U.S. Department of Housing and Urban Development website at http://www.hud.gov or call 1-800-569-4287 for information in English and Spanish. For information about buying a home and getting a mortgage, visit the Federal Citizen Information Center at http://www.pueblo.gsa.gov. See also the "For Homeowners and Home Buyers" section of http://www.fanniemae.com.

Getting a Social Security Number

As a permanent resident, you can get a Social Security number (SSN). A Social Security number is a number assigned to you by the United States government. It helps the government keep track of your earnings and the benefits you can get. It is also used by banks and other agencies, such as schools, to identify you. You may be asked for your SSN when you rent an apartment or buy a home.

The government department in charge of Social Security is called the Social Security Administration.

Find the Social Security office closest to you by:

- Asking friends or neighbors where to find the nearest Social Security office.

- Calling 1-800-772-1213 between 7 AM and 7 PM. Information is given in English and Spanish. Free interpreter services are available.

- Looking for the address in the blue pages of the phone book.

- Looking on the Social Security Administration website at http://www.socialsecurity.gov.

IF YOU DO NOT SPEAK ENGLISH

The Social Security office can provide an interpreter free of charge to help you apply for a Social Security number. Tell the person who answers the phone at 1-800-772-1213 that you don't speak English. They will find an interpreter to help on the phone. You can also get help from an interpreter when you visit the Social Security office.

The Social Security Administration website contains helpful information for people new to the United States. A section of the website has information about Social Security in 14 languages. Visit http://www.socialsecurity.gov.

You do <u>not</u> need to fill out an application or go to a Social Security office to get a Social Security number if:

- You asked for a Social Security number or card when you applied for an immigrant visa AND

- You applied for an immigrant visa in October 2002 or later AND

- You were age 18 or older when you came to the United States.

AVOID IDENTITY THEFT

"Identity theft" means someone has stolen your personal information, such as your Social Security or bank account number. They can use it to take money from your bank account or get a credit card in your name. Identity theft is a serious crime. Protect yourself by:

- Making sure you know and trust the people or businesses you give your personal information to, especially on the phone or Internet.

- Leaving your Social Security card at home in a safe place. Do not carry it with you.

- Carrying with you only the identification documents or credit cards you need at the time. Leave the rest at home in a safe place.

- Tearing up or shredding any paper or forms with your personal information on them before throwing them in the trash.

If you have a problem with identity theft, you can get help by calling the Federal Trade Commission's ID Theft Hotline at 1-877-438-4338. You also can get information at http://www.consumer.gov/idtheft.

In this situation, the information needed to assign you an SSN was sent by the Departments of State and Homeland Security to the Social Security Administration. The Social Security Administration will assign you an SSN and mail your SSN card to the same U.S. mailing address where USCIS sends your Permanent Resident Card. You should get your SSN card within 3 weeks after you arrive in the U.S. Contact the Social Security Administration if you do not get your card within 3 weeks after coming to the U.S. or if you change your mailing address after you come to the U.S. but before you receive your SSN card.

You <u>must</u> go to a Social Security office to get an SSN if:

• You did not ask for a Social Security number or card when you applied for an immigrant visa OR

• You applied for your immigrant visa before October 2002 OR

• You were under age 18 when you came to the U.S.

A Social Security representative will help you apply for an SSN. Bring these documents with you when you go to the office to apply:

• A birth certificate or other document such as your passport showing when and where you were born AND

• A document showing your immigration status, including your permission to work in the U.S. This can be your Permanent Resident Card or passport with an immigration stamp or visa label.

Your Social Security number will be sent to you in the mail. You should get your Social Security card about 2 weeks after the Social Security Administration has all documents needed for your application. If they need to verify any of your documents, it may take longer to get your SSN.

Taking Care of Your Money

Getting a Bank Account

A bank account is a safe place to keep your money. Banks have different kinds of accounts. Checking accounts (for paying bills) and savings accounts (for earning interest on your money) are two common ones. You can open an account for yourself or a joint account with your spouse or another person. Banks may charge you fees for some of their services.

Credit unions and savings and loan associations are other choices for banking. Your employer may have a credit union that you can join. Credit unions provide most of the same services as banks, but many offer extra services. Compare the services, fees, hours, and locations of banks before you open an account, so you can choose one that best meets your needs.

► TIP: Many stores offer check-cashing services and overseas money-wiring services, but these cost money. Check to see if your bank offers these services at a lower cost.

KEEPING YOUR MONEY SAFE

It is not safe to leave large amounts of money in your house. It is also not safe to carry around large amounts of cash. It could be stolen or lost. Your money is protected if you put it in a bank that is a member of the Federal Deposit Insurance Corporation (FDIC). The FDIC provides banks with insurance to protect your money. If your bank closes, the FDIC will pay you the amount of the money in your account up to $100,000. Make sure the bank you choose has FDIC insurance.

When you open a bank account, you will be asked to prove your identity. You can use your Permanent Resident Card or driver's license. You will also need to give the bank some money—called a "deposit"—to put into your new account. After a few days, you can take money out of your account. This is called "withdrawing" money. You can withdraw money by writing a check, going to an Automatic Teller Machine (ATM), or filling out a withdrawal form in the bank.

Using Your Bank Account

You can get money from your bank account using a personal check or ATM card. Be sure that only you and, if you have one, your joint account holder have access to your account.

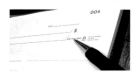

Personal checks. You will get a supply of personal checks when you open your checking account. These checks are forms that you fill out to pay for something. Checks tell your bank to pay the person or business you have written on the check. Keep these checks in a safe place.

ATM cards. You can ask your bank for an ATM card. This is a small plastic card linked to your bank account. Use this card to get cash or deposit money in your account at an ATM machine. Usually you do not pay a fee for using your own bank's ATM. You may pay a fee if you use an ATM at another bank.

The bank staff will show you how to use an ATM card and give you a special number, called a PIN ("personal identification number") to use at the ATM. Be careful when using ATMs. Never give anyone your PIN number or ATM card. They could use it to take money out of your account.

Debit cards. Your bank may give you a debit card to use for your checking account. Sometimes your ATM card can also be used as a debit card. Debit cards allow you to pay for something without writing a check by having your bank send the money directly to the business you are buying from.

Bank checks. Bank checks are checks that the bank makes out at your request. You give the bank money and they make out a bank check for that amount of money to the person or business you want to send it to. Banks may charge a fee for bank checks.

CREDIT CARDS

Credit cards—also called "charge cards"—allow you to make purchases and pay for them later. Banks, stores, and gas stations are some businesses that can give you a credit card. You get a bill in the mail each month for purchases you have made with your credit card. If you pay the entire amount on the bill when you get it, you do not have to pay interest. If you do not pay the entire amount or if you send your payment late, you will be charged interest and possibly an additional fee. Some credit cards have very high interest rates.

Be careful about giving your credit card number to others, especially over the phone or on the Internet. Be sure you know and trust the person or business that asks for your number.

TIP: Check your credit card bill each month to make sure all the charges are correct. If you see a charge that you did not make, call the credit card company immediately. You usually do not have to pay for charges you did not make if you tell the credit card company right away.

Write down the numbers for all bank accounts and debit, ATM, and credit cards. Also write down the phone numbers of these companies. Keep this information in a safe place. If your wallet is lost or stolen, you can call the companies and cancel all your cards. This will keep someone else from using your cards illegally.

YOUR CREDIT RATING

In the U.S., the way you handle your credit is very important. There are organizations that create a "credit score" or "credit rating" for you depending on how you pay bills, how many loans you take out, and other factors. This credit rating is very important when you want to buy a home or car or take out a loan. Here are some things you can do to get a good credit rating:

- Pay all your bills on time.

- Keep your credit card balances low. Pay at least the minimum amount due each month.

- Don't apply for a lot of loans or credit cards.

Under federal law, you can get one free credit report once a year. If you would like to get a copy of your credit rating report, you can call 1-877-322-8228 or go to http://www.annualcreditreport.com. Depending on what state you live in, you may not be able to get the free report until September 1, 2005. This is when people all over the U.S. can get a free credit report.

Looking for a Job

There are many ways to look for a job in the United States. To increase your chances of finding a job, you can:

- Ask friends, neighbors, family, or others in your community about job openings or good places to work.

- Look in the newspaper "Classifieds" section under "Employment."

- Look for "Help Wanted" signs in the windows of local businesses.

- Go to the Employment or Human Resources offices of businesses in your area to ask about job openings.

- Visit community agencies that help immigrants find jobs or job training programs.

- Check bulletin boards in local libraries, grocery stores, and community centers for notices of job openings.

- Check with the department of employment services for your state.

- Search for jobs on the Internet. If you are using a computer at your library, the library staff can help you get started.

Applying for a Job

Most employers will ask you to fill out a job application. This is a form with questions about your address, education, and past work experience. It may also ask for information about people you have worked with in the past. These are called "references," and the employer may want to call them to ask questions about you.

You may need to create a "resumé" with a list of your work experience. A resumé tells your employer about your past jobs, your education or training, and your job skills. Take your resumé when you apply for work.

A good resumé:

- Has your name, address, and phone number.

- Lists your past jobs and includes dates you worked.

- Shows your level of education.

- Shows any special skills you have.

- Is easy to read and has no mistakes.

Check with local community service agencies to see if they can help you write a resumé. Private businesses can help with this, too, but they charge a fee.

The Job Interview

Employers may want to meet with you to talk about the job. They will ask about your past work and your skills. You can practice answering questions about your past work and your skills with a friend or family member so you will be ready. You can also ask questions of the employer. This is a good chance to find out about the job.

WHAT ARE BENEFITS?

In addition to your pay, some employers provide extra employment "benefits." Benefits may include:

- Medical care.
- Dental care.
- Eye care.
- Life insurance.
- Retirement plan.

Employers may pay some or all of the costs of these benefits. Ask about the benefits your employer will provide.

You may want to ask:

- What are the hours of work?

- How much does the job pay? (U.S. law requires most employers to pay a "minimum wage," which is the lowest wage permitted.)

- How many vacation days are there?

- How many sick days are there?

- What benefits come with the job?

During the interview, an employer can ask you many questions. But employers are not allowed to ask some questions. No one should ask you about your race,

KNOW YOUR RIGHTS: FEDERAL LAWS PROTECT EMPLOYEES

Several federal laws forbid employers from discriminating against people looking for a job. The United States has laws forbidding discrimination because of:

- Race, color, religion, country of origin, and sex (Civil Rights Act).

- Age (Age Discrimination in Employment Act).

- Disabilities (Americans with Disabilities Act).

- Sex (Equal Pay Act).

For more information about these protections, visit the U.S. Equal Employment Opportunity Commission website at http://www.eeoc.gov or call 1-800-669-4000 and 1-800-669-6820 (for hearing impaired).

Other laws help keep work places safe, provide for leave in cases of family or medical emergencies, and provide temporary funds for unemployed workers. Visit the U.S. Department of Labor website at http://www.dol.gov for more information about workers' rights.

color, sex, marriage, religion, country of origin, age, or any disability you may have.

What to Expect When You Are Hired
When you go to your new job for the first time, you will be asked to fill out some forms. These include:

- Form I-9, the Employment Eligibility Verification Form. By law, your employer must check to see that all newly hired workers are eligible to work in the U.S. On your first day of work, you will need to fill in the I-9 form. Within 3 business days, you must show your employer your identity documents and work authorization documents. You can choose what documents to show as proof of your right to work in the U.S., as long as the document is listed on the I-9 form. The list of acceptable documents is on the back of the I-9 form. Examples of acceptable documents are your Permanent Resident Card or an unrestricted Social Security number card in combination with a state-issued driver's license.

- Form W-4, Employee's Withholding Allowance Certificate. Your employer should take federal taxes from your paycheck to send to the government. This is called "withholding tax." Form W-4 tells your employer to withhold taxes and helps you figure out the right amount to withhold.

- Other Forms. You may also need to fill out a tax withholding form for the state you live in and forms so that you can get benefits.

You may be paid each week, every two weeks, or once a month. Your paycheck will show the amount taken out for federal and state taxes, Social Security taxes, and any employment benefits you pay. Some employers will send your pay directly to your bank; this is called "direct deposit."

Speaking English at Work

If you do not speak English, try to learn it as soon as possible. You can find free or low-cost English language classes in your community, often through the local public schools or community college. Knowing English will help you in your job, your community, and your daily life. See page 60 for more information on learning English.

FEDERAL PROTECTION FOR IMMIGRANT WORKERS

Federal law says that employers cannot discriminate against you because of your immigration status. Employers cannot:

- Refuse to hire you, or fire you, because of your immigration status or because you are not a U.S. citizen.

- Require you to show a Permanent Resident Card, or reject your lawful work papers.

- Prefer hiring undocumented workers.

- Discriminate against you because of your national origin (or country of origin).

- Retaliate against any employee who complains of the above treatment.

For more information about your rights, or to file a complaint, call the Office of Special Counsel at 1-800-255-7688 or 1-800-237-2515 (for hearing impaired). If you do not speak English, interpreters are available to help you. You also can visit http://www.usdoj.gov/crt/osc for more information.

If your employer says you <u>must</u> speak English at work, he or she must show that speaking English is required for you to do your job correctly. Your employer must also tell you that English is required before you are hired. If your employer cannot show that speaking English is required for your job, he or she may be breaking a federal law. If you need assistance or more information, you can contact the U.S. Equal Employment Opportunity Commission (EEOC). Call 1-800-669-4000 or 1-800-669-6820 (hearing impaired) or go to <u>http://www.eeoc.gov</u>.

Drug Tests and Background Checks

For some jobs, you may be required to take a test to make sure you are not using illegal drugs. Some jobs require that you have a background check, an investigation into your past activities and present circumstances.

Paying Taxes

Taxes are money paid by U.S. citizens and residents to federal, state, and local governments. Taxes pay for services provided by the government. There are different types of taxes, such as income tax, sales tax, and property tax.

Income tax. Income tax is paid to federal, most state, and some local governments. "Taxable income" is money that you get from wages, self-employment, tips, and the sale of property. Most people pay income taxes by having money withheld from their paycheck. The amount of income tax you must pay depends on how much you earn. Income tax rates are lower for people who make less money. Anyone who earns income, resides in the United States, and meets certain requirements needs to file a tax return and pay any taxes they owe.

The Internal Revenue Service (IRS) is the federal agency that collects income tax. Taxpayers file a federal "income tax return" Form 1040 with the IRS each year. Your tax return tells the government how much you earned and how much in taxes was taken out of your paycheck. If you had too much taken out of your paycheck, you will get a refund. If you did not have enough taken out of your paycheck, you must send a payment to the IRS.

Social Security and Medicare taxes. These federal taxes are withheld from your paycheck. Social Security provides benefits for certain retired workers and their families; certain disabled workers and their families; and certain family members of deceased workers. Medicare taxes pay for medical services for most people over age 65. In most cases, you must work a total of 10 years (or 40 quarters) over the course of your life to get Social Security retirement benefits and Medicare benefits. You may need fewer than 10 years of work to get disability benefits or for your family to get survivors' benefits based on your earnings.

Sales taxes. Sales taxes are state and local taxes. These taxes are added to the cost of buying certain things. Sales taxes are based on the cost of the item. Sales taxes help pay for services provided by state and local government, such as roads, police, and firemen.

Property taxes. These are state and local taxes on your house and land. In most places, property taxes help support local public schools and other services.

YOUR W-2 FORM: WAGE AND TAX STATEMENT

A W-2 is a federal form that lists your earnings and the taxes you paid for the last tax year. A tax year is from January 1 to December 31 of each year. By law, your employer must send you a W-2 form by January 31 each year. You will receive a W-2 form for each job you have. You must send a copy of your W-2 form with your federal income tax return to the IRS. If you live or work in a state that collects income tax, you must send a copy of your W-2 with your state income tax return.

Getting Help With Your Taxes

As a permanent resident, you are required to file a federal income tax return every year. This return covers your earnings for January to December of the past year. You must file your return by April 15. You can get free help with your tax return at an IRS Taxpayer Assistance Center. You don't need to call ahead.

Taxpayer Assistance Centers are located in communities across the United States. To find the Taxpayer Assistance Center where you live, visit http://www.irs.gov/localcontacts/index.html. To get help by phone, call the IRS at 1-800-829-1040.

HOW GOVERNMENT WORKS FOR US

Taxes pay for the services the federal government provides to the people of the United States. Some examples of these services are:

- Keeping our country safe and secure.
- Curing and preventing diseases through research.
- Protecting our money in banks by insuring it.
- Educating children and adults.
- Building and maintaining our roads and highways.
- Providing medical services for the poor and elderly.
- Giving emergency help when natural disasters strike, such as hurricanes, floods, or earthquakes.

Traveling in the United States

There are many ways to travel in the United States. Many cities have buses, trains (also called "subways"), trolleys, or streetcars. Anyone can ride these vehicles for a small fee. In some places, you can buy a card good for several trips on subways or buses. You can also pay for each trip separately. Taxicabs, or "taxis," are cars that take you where you want to go for a fee. Taxis are more expensive than other types of public transportation.

Getting a Driver's License

It is against the law to drive without a driver's license. You must apply for and get a driver's license if you want to drive. You get your driver's license from the state where you live.

Check with the state office that issues driver's licenses to find out how to get one. These offices have different names in each state. Some common names are Department of Motor Vehicles, Department of Transportation, Motor Vehicle Administration, or Department of Public Safety. You can find these offices in the blue pages of the phone book or get more

SHOULD I BUY A CAR?

Owning a car can be a convenient way to get around. In the U.S., you must also pay for car insurance, registering your vehicle, and licenses. Heavy traffic can make driving difficult in some cities. Think of all the costs and benefits before you decide to buy a car.

information at http://www.firstgov.gov/Topics/
Motor_Vehicles.shtml.

Some permanent residents already have a driver's license from another country. You may be able to trade this for a license in your state. Check with your state office to see if you can do this.

10 TIPS FOR DRIVING SAFELY IN THE U.S.

- Drive on the right-hand side of the road.

- Always have your driver's license and insurance card with you.

- Always wear your seat belt.

- Use proper seat belts and car safety seats for children.

- Use your car's signals to show if you are turning left or right.

- Obey all traffic laws and signals.

- Pull over to the side of the road if an emergency vehicle—police car, fire truck, or ambulance—needs to pass you.

- Do not pass a school bus when its red lights are flashing.

- Do not drive if you have been drinking or taking drugs.

- Be very careful when driving in fog, ice, rain, or snow.

TIP: A driver's license is used for identification in the United States. It's a good idea to get one even if you don't own a car.

If you do not know how to drive, you can take driving lessons. Many public school districts have classes in "driver education." You can also look under "Driving Instruction" in the yellow pages of the phone book.

TIP: Hitchhiking is not common in the United States. In many places, it is illegal. For safety reasons, do not hitchhike and do not give rides to hitchhikers.

TRAVEL INFORMATION

For bus travel:
Greyhound 1-800-229-9424 or
http://www.greyhound.com.

For train travel:
Amtrak 1-800-872-7245 or
http://www.amtrak.com.

For air travel: There are many airlines in the U.S. Look in your phone book yellow pages under "Airlines."

Taking Care of Your Health

People in the U.S. pay for their own medical care. Medical care is expensive, so many people buy health insurance. You should get health insurance for yourself and your family as soon as possible.

Employers may offer health insurance as a benefit to their employees. Some employers pay all of your monthly health insurance fee, and some pay only part of the fee. This monthly fee is called a "premium." You may need to pay part of the premium. Usually, employers will deduct the employee's part of the premium from their paycheck.

Doctors send their bills to your health insurance company. The health insurance company will pay for some or all of your medical services. Often you must pay a portion of your medical bills. This is sometimes called a "co-payment."

If you do not have health insurance, you may be able to get federal or state healthcare assistance. In general, most states provide some type of assistance to children

FINDING A CLINIC OR OTHER LOW-COST HEALTHCARE

Clinics are medical offices that provide free or low-cost services. Most communities have at least one clinic. Community organizations that work with immigrants may know of a low-cost or free clinic in your area.

The U.S. Department of Health and Human Services also provides basic healthcare to immigrants. They have a website that lists clinics and other healthcare choices. To find a clinic or doctor near you, visit http://ask.hrsa.gov/pc/ . Type in your state or zip code to get the information. You can also look in the yellow pages under "Social Services."

and pregnant women. Check with the public health department of your state or town.

If you need urgent medical care, you can go to the emergency room of the nearest hospital. Most hospitals are required by federal law to treat patients with a medical emergency even if the person cannot pay.

Federal and State Health Programs

Medicaid is a joint federal/state program for low-income people. Each state has its own Medicaid guidelines. Medicaid pays for medical services, such as visits to the doctor and hospitalization. Permanent residents who entered the U.S. <u>before</u> August 22, 1996 may be able to get Medicaid if they meet certain conditions. Permanent residents who entered the U.S. <u>on or after</u> August 22, 1996 may be able to get Medicaid if they have lived in the U.S. for 5 years or longer and meet certain conditions.

Medicare is a health insurance program for people 65 years of age or older or who have specific disabilities. Medicare pays for services if you are sick or injured, but does not pay for routine care (such as check-ups with your doctor), dental care, or eye care. Medicare allows the use of discount drug cards for people enrolled in Medicare. These cards may help you save money when you buy prescription drugs. If you are eligible for Medicare, you may be able to get one of these discount cards.

MORE INFORMATION ABOUT MEDICAID AND MEDICARE

Contact the Social Security Administration at 1-800-772-1213 or the Centers for Medicare and Medicaid Service website at http://www.cms.hhs.gov.

Medicare has two parts, Part A and Part B. Part A is free and pays for hospital care and nursing homes certified by Medicare. Part B pays for visits to the doctor, ambulances, tests, and outpatient hospital care. For Part B, you pay a monthly fee.

Permanent residents can get Medicare Part A and Part B if they meet certain conditions. Those who are 65 and older are automatically in Medicare when they start getting Social Security retirement benefits. If you are not 65 but are eligible for other reasons, call the Social Security office near you for information about enrolling. Generally, you must have worked in the U.S. for 10 years (or 40

quarters) over the course of your life to get these Medicare benefits.

State Children's Health Insurance Program (SCHIP)
Your children may be able to get free or low-cost healthcare if you meet certain conditions. Every state has a health insurance program for infants, children, and teenagers. The insurance pays for doctor visits, prescription medicines, hospital care, and other healthcare services. In most states, children 18 and younger without health insurance whose families meet certain income limits are eligible. Children can get free or low-cost healthcare without affecting their parents' immigration status.

MORE INFORMATION ABOUT SCHIP

Each state has its own SCHIP rules. You need to find out about the program in your state. For information about SCHIP in your state, call **1-877-543-7669** or visit http://www.insurekidsnow.gov and enter the name of your state.

Other Federal Benefits Programs

You or members of your family may be eligible for other federal benefits, depending on your immigration status, length of time in the U.S., and income.

The Food Stamp Program
Some low-income immigrants and immigrant children may be eligible for food stamp assistance,  depending on their immigration status, length of time in the U.S., and income. Food stamps allow you to obtain some foods free at grocery stores. Some states may have their own state-funded food stamp programs with different rules for eligibility. For information on federal food stamp eligibility from the U.S. Food and Nutrition Service in 34 different languages, visit http://www.fns.usda.gov/fsp/outreach/translations.htm.

Services for Survivors of Domestic Violence
Immigrants and their children who are survivors of domestic violence may be eligible for federal benefits and services, such as battered women's shelters or food stamps. For more information on these services from the U.S. Department of Health and Human Services, visit http://www.hhs.gov/ocr/immigration/bifsltr.html.

Temporary Assistance for Needy Families (TANF)
Temporary Assistance for Needy Families is a federal program that gives money to states to provide assistance and  work opportunities for low-income families. Immigrants may be eligible, depending on their immigration status, length of time in the U.S., and income. Programs differ by state and some states have their own state-funded assistance program. For links and information on TANF, visit http://www.acf.dhhs.gov/programs/ofa/.

Assistance for Disabled Immigrants

Immigrants with disabilities may be eligible for Medicaid, food stamps, and Supplemental Security Income, depending upon their immigration status, length of time in the U.S., and income. For more information on food stamps, see page 47. For information about Supplemental Security Income, see http://www.ssa.gov/notices/supplemental-security-income/spotlights/spot-non-citizens.htm.

One-Stop Career Centers

The federal government funds career centers that offer training referrals, career counseling, job listings, and other employment-related services. English as a Second Language (ESL) classes and job skills training are also offered to immigrants, depending on their immigration status and income, at some of these centers. For information on One-Stop Career Centers throughout the U.S., visit http://www.doleta.gov/usworkforce/onestop/onestopmap.cfm.

TIP: You can visit http://www.govbenefits.gov to find out about services that might be available to you.

Education and Childcare

Education can help connect you and your family to your community. This section describes schools in the United States for children, youth, and adults and answers questions you may have about them. It also offers suggestions for finding good childcare, if you have young children at home and need to work.

Education

To make sure all children are prepared to succeed, the U.S. provides free public education. This section tells you how to sign your children up for school. You will learn how U.S. schools work and how to help your children learn.

Enrolling Your Child in School

Most public schools in the United States are co-educational. Co-educational means that girls and boys attend classes together. The United States has compulsory school attendance laws. This means that state laws require all children ages 5 to 16 to attend school in most states. Check with your state department of education to find out the required ages for school attendance in your state.

You can send your child to a public or private school. In most states, parents may also teach their children at home. This is called "home schooling." Public schools are free and do not offer religious instruction. What your children learn in public school is set by the state. However, local teachers and parents decide how it is taught. Your federal and state income taxes and your local property taxes pay for these schools.

Students must pay a fee (called "tuition") to attend private schools. Religious groups run many private schools. Some are co-educational. Some are only for boys or only for girls. Some offer financial help for students who cannot pay the tuition.

Most American children are in school for 12 years. Your children will be placed in a class (called a "grade") based on their age and how much previous education they have. Sometimes a school may give your child a test to decide what grade he or she should be in.

HOW MOST U.S. SCHOOLS ARE ORGANIZED

Elementary or Primary School
Kindergarten and Grades 1 to 5
Children Ages 5 to 10

Junior or Middle School
Grades 6 to 8
Youth Ages 11 to 13

Secondary or High School
Grades 9 to 12
Young Adults Ages 14 to 18

**Postsecondary or
Higher Education,
Public and Private
Community Colleges,
2-year or 4-year Colleges or
Universities, Trade Schools
All Adults May Attend**

One of the first things you should do is enroll your child in school. Some questions that parents often ask about public schools include:

Q: **How long is the school year?**

A: The school year usually begins in August or September and ends in May or June. In some places, children attend school all year. Children are in school Monday through Friday. Some schools offer programs before or after regular school hours for children whose parents work. You may be charged a fee for these programs.

Q: **Where do I enroll my child?**

A: Call or visit your local school district's main office to find out which school your child should attend. Tell the school staff your child's age and the address where you live.

Q: What documents do I need to enroll my child?

A: You need your child's medical records and proof that they have certain immunizations (also called "shots") to protect them from disease. You also may need proof that you live in the same community as the school. If you have lost these documents, ask school staff how to get new documents. To avoid delays, do this before you try to enroll your child.

Q: What if my child does not speak English?

A: The school is responsible for testing and placing your child in the right program. Schools receive state and federal funds for programs and services like English as a Second Language (ESL) and bilingual education. You can call your child's school to ask about testing, placement, and services. Even if your child does not speak English, he or she needs to learn the academic material for his or her grade level. This can happen through ESL or bilingual education.

Q: What if my child is disabled?

A: Students with a physical or mental disability can get a free public education, just like a child who does not have a disability. Your child will be placed in a regular school classroom, if possible. If your child's disability is severe, he or she may be given special education services outside the regular classroom.

Q: My child was not in school before coming to the United States. How long can he or she attend public school for free?

A: Your child can attend school for free until they reach age 21 in most states. If your child has not graduated from high school by then, he or she can enroll in adult education classes to obtain a General Educational Development (GED) certificate instead of a high school diploma. Call your local school district office or your state department of education to find out where GED classes are offered.

Q: How will my child get to school?

A: Children can sometimes walk to school in the United States. If the school is too far away, they will ride a bus. Public schools have buses, which are free. Students are picked up and dropped off at a school-bus stop near your home. To find out if your child can ride the bus, contact your local school system. If you have a car, you can also set up a "car pool" with other parents in your area to share driving your children to school.

Q: What will my child eat at school?

A: Children can take lunch to school or buy it at the school cafeteria. The U.S. government also provides nutritious free or low-cost breakfast and lunch for children who cannot afford to buy food at school. Call or visit your child's school to find out if it participates in the federal School Meals program. Talk with school staff to find out if your children are eligible to participate.

FEDERAL SCHOOL MEALS PROGRAM

Children learn better when they are well fed. To improve learning, the United States government provides healthy low-cost or free meals to more than 26 million children each school day. Participation in the **School Breakfast Program** and **National School Lunch Program** is based on family income and size. The **Special Milk Program** provides milk to children who do not participate in other federal school meals programs. For more information about these programs, visit the U.S. Department of Agriculture website at http://www.fns.usda.gov/cnd/.

Q: **Who pays for books and school activities?**

A: Public schools usually provide free books. Students must usually buy their own school supplies, such as paper and pencils. If you cannot pay for these supplies, contact your child's school. Some schools may charge a small fee for supplies or special events, such as school trips. Many schools offer after-school sports and music programs. You may need to pay a fee for your children to participate in some of these programs.

Q: **What will my child learn?**

A: Each state sets academic standards for schools. These standards state what all students should know and be able to do. Local school districts decide how this information should be taught. Most schools teach English, math, social studies, science, and physical education. Art, music, and foreign languages are sometimes offered.

Q: **How is my child's work judged?**

A: Teachers assign grades based on the work your child does during the school year. Grades are usually based on homework, tests, attendance, and class behavior. You will receive a "report card" several times a year. This report card tells you how your child is doing in each subject. Schools have different ways of grading students. Some use letter grades, with A or A+ for excellent work and D or F for poor or failing work. Others use number grades. Others summarize your child's performance with words like "excellent," "good," or "needs improvement." Ask school staff how students in your child's school are graded.

Q: How can I talk to my child's teacher?

A: Most schools have regular parent conferences for you to meet with your child's teacher. You can also schedule meetings to talk with teachers or school administrators about how your child is doing in school. If you do not speak English, ask if there is someone at the school who speaks your language and can help interpret.

Q: What if my child misses school?

A: Being in school is very important. Parents must send a written letter to the teacher or call the school to explain why their child was not in school. Let the teacher know in advance if your child will be out of school. Students must usually make up any work they missed.

WHAT YOU CAN DO

Most public and private schools have a Parent Teacher Association (PTA) or Parent Teacher Organization (PTO). These groups help parents learn about what is going on in their child's school and how to get involved in school events. Anyone can join, even grandparents. The PTA/PTOs also support schools by sponsoring special activities and by providing volunteers to help out in the classroom. You can get involved even if you do not speak much English. Many schools have information specifically for parents with limited English-speaking skills. Call or visit your school office to find out when the PTA/PTO for your child's school meets and how you can join.

Q: **What if my child gets into trouble?**

A: Many schools have a list of rules that students must obey. These are called "codes of conduct." Ask your child's school about its code of conduct. Students who break school rules may be punished by being required to stay after the school day is over. Or they may not be allowed to participate in sports or other school activities. Physical punishment is NOT permitted in most U.S. schools.

Children may be suspended or expelled from school if they behave very badly and break school rules often. Your child will no longer be able to go to school if he or she is expelled. You will need to meet with school staff to find out how to get your child back in school.

Q: **Is my child safe in school?**

A: Most American public schools are safe places to learn. But some schools—mainly high schools— have problems with violence, street gangs, or drugs and alcohol. Talk to a teacher, school counselor, or administrator if you are worried about your child's safety.

Higher Education: Colleges and Universities

Young adults can continue their education in a 2-year community or technical college or a 4-year college or university after high school. These are called "postsecondary institutions" or "institutions of higher education." There are public and private institutions of higher education. Public colleges and universities cost less than private ones, especially for residents of the state where the college or university is located. Young adults can also choose to attend schools to learn specific jobs, such as repairing computers or being a healthcare assistant.

Students in higher education choose a specific subject to study in depth (this subject is called their "major"). Choosing a major helps prepare them for employment or further education in that field.

Degree Type	Type of School	Years of Schooling
Certificate	Community College/ Trade School	6 months to 2 years
Associate's	Community College	2 years
Bachelor's	4-year College or University	4 years
Master's	University	2 years
Doctorate	University	2–8 years
Professional	Specialized School	2–5 years

A college or university education can be expensive. Some schools provide financial help called "scholarships." The U.S. government also provides financial aid for students. Most students take out a loan or apply for financial aid or scholarships to help pay for their schooling.

Federal Financial Aid for College Students

The U.S. government provides financial help to students attending certain institutions of higher education. This aid covers many school expenses, including tuition, fees, books, room and board, supplies, and transportation. Students qualify for this aid by their financial need, not their grades. There are three types of federal aid:

- Grants—money that you don't have to repay.

- Work Study—money that you earn while you are in school.

- Loans—money that you borrow that you must repay later with interest.

For more information on federal financial aid programs, call 1-800-433-3243 or visit the U.S. Department of Education website http://www.studentaid.ed.gov/students/publications/student_guide/index.html. Information is also available in Spanish.

BEWARE OF FINANCIAL AID FRAUD

Be careful when you are searching for information on student financial assistance. Avoid offers that seem too good to be true or that promise you results in exchange for money. Every year, families lose millions of dollars to "scholarship fraud." If you are the victim of fraud, or for free information, call 1-877-382-4357 or 1-866-653-4261 for hearing impaired, or visit the Federal Trade Commission website at http://www.ftc.gov/scholarshipscams.

Adult Education

Learning does not have to end when you become an adult. In the U.S., people are encouraged to become "lifelong learners." If you are 16 years of age or older and have not completed high school, you can enroll in Adult Secondary Education (ASE) classes. These classes prepare you to earn a General Educational Development (GED) certificate.

A GED certificate is an alternative high school diploma. It shows that you have learned high-school-level academic knowledge and skills. To earn a GED, you must take and pass tests in 5 different areas: reading, writing, social studies, science, and mathematics. Most U.S. employers consider a GED credential to be equal to a regular high school diploma. In many areas, GED preparation classes are free or low-cost. Look in the phone book under "Adult Education" or call your local school district office for information.

Many adults take classes to learn more about a subject that interests them or to learn new skills that can help them in their jobs. Many public school systems and local community colleges offer classes in a wide range of subjects for adults. Anyone can enroll in these classes, which generally have low fees. Check with your local school system or community college to find out what classes are available, how much they cost, and how to enroll.

Learning English

There are many places where you can learn how to speak, read, and write in English. Many children and adults enroll in English as a Second Language (ESL) classes. These classes help people who do not know English to learn the language. These classes are also called English for Speakers of Other Languages (ESOL) or English Literacy classes.

Children who do not know English will learn it in school. America's public schools provide help and instruction for all students who need to learn English. Students who need extra help are often called Limited English Proficient (LEP) students.

Students just beginning to learn English may take an ESL class in place of a regular English class. Students with more English language skills may be placed in a regular classroom and given extra help. Some schools also offer after-school programs and tutoring to help students learn English. Your child's school will tell you what kind of help they give students who need to learn English.

Adults who do not understand English can enroll in an ESL class offered in a public adult and community education program or private language school.

Public adult and community education programs are often offered in local communities by school districts and community colleges. These programs may provide ESL classes along with tutoring from local volunteers. These programs are often free, or you may pay a small fee. Classes may meet during day or evening hours. Call your local community college or school district office to find the nearest ESL program. Look in the blue pages of your phone book under the heading "Schools—Public."

Most large cities also have private language schools that offer day or evening ESL classes. The cost for these classes is often based on the number of hours of instruction. Private language classes are generally more expensive than public classes. To find a private language school, look in the yellow pages of your telephone book under the heading "Language Schools."

Some community organizations, libraries, and religious groups also offer free or low-cost ESL classes. Check with your local public library, social service agency, or place of worship. The reference librarian at the local library can also tell you about ESL programs and show you where to find ESL books, tapes, CDs, and computer software at the library.

CALL 211 FOR INFORMATION ON SOCIAL SERVICES

You can now call 211 in many states to get help finding the services you need. Call 211 to find out where you can enroll in ESL classes in your neighborhood. You can also call 211 if you need help finding food, housing, a drug treatment program, or other social services.

Some states and counties do not yet offer 211 services. If you call and get no answer, this 211 service is not yet available in your community.

Childcare

If you work and your children are too young to go to school, you may need to find someone to watch them while you are at work. Sometimes children in school need someone to watch them when school is over, if their parents cannot be at home. If you or other family members are not able to watch your children, you need to find someone to take care of them. Do not leave young children at home alone.

Finding Childcare

Choosing someone to care for your children is an important decision. As you make this decision, think about the quality and cost of care. Try to find a caregiver who is close to your home or job.

There are many resources you can use to find a good childcare provider. Ask other parents, friends, and co-workers who cares for their children. Some states have a childcare referral agency that can give you a list of state-licensed childcare programs. Licensed childcare programs meet specific requirements set by the state for the protection of your children. You also can call your local school district office to find places where other children in your neighborhood are cared for.

► TIP: If you need help finding good childcare in your area, the U.S. Department of Health and Human Services has a National Child Care Information Center. Call 1-800-616-2242 for information. You can also find information and answers to questions about how to choose a good program for your child at http://www.childcareaware.org.

TYPES OF CHILDCARE

You have a number of choices when choosing a childcare provider.

In-Home Care. A caregiver comes into your home to watch your children. This type of service can be expensive, because your child gets more individual attention. The quality of care depends on the person you hire.

Family Childcare. Your child is cared for in somebody else's home with a small group of other children. This can be less expensive than other types of childcare. The quality of care depends on the people who watch your child and the number of children they are caring for in their home.

Daycare Centers: Daycare centers are programs located in schools, churches or other faith-based organizations, and other places. Centers usually have several caregivers who watch larger groups of children. Centers must meet state standards and their staff usually have special training and experience.

Head Start Programs: The federal government provides funding for "Early Head Start" and "Head Start" programs for low-income families. These programs provide care and educational services to young children to get them ready for school. To learn more about these programs, call the Department of Health and Human Services at 1-866-763-6481 or visit the website http://www.acf.hhs.gov/programs/hsb/ .

Some childcare providers will take care of children for a full day or only part of the day, depending on the parents' needs. Cost is also a factor in choosing a caregiver. Check to see if you are eligible for federal or state childcare assistance. Many states offer financial assistance to low-income parents who are working or participating in job training or education programs.

▶ TIP: Make sure the childcare provider or program you are using is licensed or accredited. "Licensed" means that the program meets minimum safety and care standards set by the state. "Accredited" programs meet higher standards than those required for a state license.

How Can You Tell if a Childcare Provider Is Good? Think about these basic questions when you visit a childcare program.

• Are the children happy when around the staff?

• Are toys available that are appropriate for the children's ages?

• Were children doing an appropriate activity?

• Did the provider talk to your child while you were there?

• Is the space clean and organized?

• Is there a curriculum or routine for the children?

Be sure to ask for references so that you can talk to other parents about the program.

Emergencies and Safety

Emergencies are unexpected events that can cause harm to people and property. They can happen to anyone at any time. Plan ahead to keep yourself and your family safe. This section tells you how you can prepare for emergencies and how to get help when they happen.

Emergency Help: Call 911

In the United States, you can call 911 on any telephone to get emergency help. Call 911 to:

• Report a fire.

• Report a crime in progress.

• Call an ambulance for emergency medical help.

• Report suspicious activities, such as screams, calls for help, or gunshots.

What Happens When I Call 911?

• Calls to 911 are usually answered within 12 seconds. You may be put on hold. Do not hang up! When the operator answers, there will be silence on the phone for several seconds. Do not hang up. Wait for the operator to speak.

• If you do not speak English, tell the operator what language you speak. An interpreter should come on the line.

• The 911 operator will ask you questions to find out what and where the emergency is. Keep calm and answer these questions. Try to stay on the phone with the operator until you answer all questions.

When Not to Call 911

Call 911 for serious, life-threatening emergencies only. Calling 911 for the wrong reason may keep someone else from getting the help they need. Do not call 911 to:

- Ask for directions.

- Ask for information about public services.

- Find out if someone is in jail.

- Report situations that are not emergencies.

- Ask for information about animal control.

- Talk to a police officer about something that is not an emergency.

If you have a question for the police, call the non-emergency number for the police department listed in the blue pages of your phone book.

LAW ENFORCEMENT IN THE UNITED STATES

In the U.S., there are federal, state, and local law enforcement agencies that protect the public. In your community, law enforcement officers are the police or sheriff. Find out the phone number of the police station nearest you and keep it next to your telephone. Remember that police officers are there to protect you and your family from harm. Do not be afraid to report a crime, especially if you are the victim. Some criminals take advantage of immigrants because they think you will not report the crime to the police. If you are stopped by a police officer:

- Don't be afraid. Be polite and cooperative.

- Tell the officer if you do not speak English.

- If you are in a car, don't get out of the car until the officer tells you to.

- Keep your hands where the officer can see them. Don't reach into your pockets or into other areas of the car.

Keeping Your Home and Family Safe

Get ready before emergencies happen. Here are some things you can do to be safe:

• Be sure your doors have good locks and keep them locked at all times. Don't give your door keys to strangers. Be careful about opening your door to strangers. Ask who they are and what they want before you open the door.

• Smoke alarms make a loud noise when there is smoke in your house or apartment. Make sure you have smoke alarms on the ceiling near bedrooms and on each floor of your house. Replace the batteries in your smoke alarm twice a year. Check the alarm once each month to make sure it works.

• Find out where the nearest hospital and police and fire stations are located. Keep these important phone numbers (police station, fire department, and doctor) near your phone, where you can easily find them.

• Find the main valves for gas, electricity, and water in your home. Be sure you know how to turn them off by hand.

• Prepare a disaster kit that includes a flashlight, portable radio, extra batteries, blankets, a first-aid kit, and enough canned or packaged food and bottled water to last for 3 days. Also include trash bags, toilet paper, and pet food, if needed. Keep all these things in one place that is easy to find.

- Practice with your family how to get out of your house in case of a fire or other emergency. Make sure your children know what the smoke alarm sounds like and what to do if they hear it. Plan a place to meet your family if you have to leave your home. Choose one spot outside your home and another spot outside your neighborhood, in case you can't return home. Ask a friend or family member living in another area to be the main person your family will call if you are separated in an emergency. Make sure everyone knows to call this person and has his or her phone number.

- Ask about emergency plans at your children's school. Be sure your child knows what to do. Ask where you can go to meet your child in an emergency.

WHAT YOU CAN DO

NEIGHBORHOOD CRIME WATCH

To help keep your neighborhood safe, get to know your neighbors. Talk with them about how to handle an emergency in your area. If you have neighbors with disabilities, see if they need special help.

Many neighborhoods have a Neighborhood Watch. The Neighborhood Watch is a group of people from the neighborhood. They take turns walking the streets at night to discourage criminal activity. If there is a Neighborhood Watch in your area, you can volunteer to participate. If you want to get a Neighborhood Watch started, call your local police department for help. Visit http://www.usaonwatch.org for more information.

When you help others to be safe, you help your community and nation. You can get more involved in your community through your local Citizen Corps Council. Visit http://www.citizencorps.gov for more information.

First Aid

Learn how to help in certain emergency situations, such as when someone is bleeding or choking. This is called "first aid." You can take a first aid training class through your local Red Cross. Call your local Red Cross office or the National Safety Council to ask about classes in your area. Find more information at http://www.redcross.org or http://www.nsc.org.

Keep a first aid kit at home, at work, and in your car. A first aid kit has items you can use for small injuries or for pain, such as bandages, antiseptic wipes, pain medicine, instant ice packs, and gloves. You can buy a good first aid kit at your local drugstore.

Poison Control

Many things in your home can be poisonous if they are swallowed. These can include cleaning products, medicine, paint, alcohol, cosmetics, and even some plants. Keep these things away from young children.

If someone swallows a poisonous substance, call the Poison Control Center right away at 1-800-222-1222. You can get help 24 hours a day, 7 days a week. Have the poisonous substance with you when you call. Tell the operator what it is. If you do not speak English, tell the operator so an interpreter can help you. Calls to the Poison Control Center are confidential and free.

Homeland Security Advisory System for Terrorist Attacks

The Department of Homeland Security (DHS) has a system to help people understand the risk of a possible terrorist attack. The system uses different colors to show different levels of danger. These are:

■**Red**. Severe condition. There is a severe risk of terrorist attacks. An attack has already happened or is about to happen.

■**Orange**. High condition. There is a high risk of terrorist attacks. No specific targets are known.

■**Yellow**. Elevated condition. There is a significant risk of terrorist attacks. No specific targets are known.

■**Blue**. Guarded condition. There is a general risk of terrorist attacks. No specific threats or targets are known.

■**Green**. Low condition. There is a low risk of terrorist attacks.

If a Terrorist Attack Happens

The U.S. government can use the Emergency Alert System (EAS) to provide information to the country in an emergency. The President of the United States can use this system to provide immediate information to the public when an emergency happens. State and local governments may also use the EAS to provide emergency information to the public in their area. If an emergency happens, listen to the radio or television for information about how to protect yourself and your family.

SEVERE
SEVERE RISK OF TERRORIST ATTACKS

HIGH
HIGH RISK OF TERRORIST ATTACKS

ELEVATED
SIGNIFICANT RISK OF TERRORIST ATTACKS

GUARDED
GENERAL RISK OF TERRORIST ATTACKS

LOW
LOW RISK OF TERRORIST ATTACKS

▶ TIP: If a terrorist attack happens, listen to what local authorities tell you to do. Listen to the radio or television for instructions. Have a television or radio in your home that works on batteries in case electricity in your area is temporarily lost.

Don't Be Afraid, Be Ready

DHS is helping Americans learn about possible dangers, so they can be ready to react during a terrorist attack or natural disaster. DHS provides information to help you make your family, your home, and your community safer from the dangers of crime, terrorism, and disasters of all kinds. Call 1-800-BE-READY for printed information or visit the DHS website at http://www.ready.gov.

You can get a *Citizen's Guide* with tips on how to make your family, your home, and your community safer. You can get this guide from the Federal Emergency Management Agency (FEMA) by calling 1-800-480-2520. You also can get materials from the Citizen Corps website at http://www.citizencorps.gov/ready/cc_pubs.shtm.

WHAT YOU CAN DO

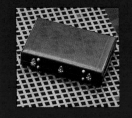

Federal and state officials are asking all people living in the U.S. to help fight terrorism. Be aware of your surroundings, especially when you travel on public buses, trains, and airplanes. If you see a suspicious item that has been left behind, such as a briefcase, backpack, or paper bag, report it immediately to the nearest police officer or other authority. Do not open or remove the item yourself!

Learning About the United States

The United States is a representative democracy, and citizens here play a very important role in governing the country. In this section, you will learn about how citizens help shape the U.S. government, how the United States began and developed, and how our government operates.

We the People: The Role of the Citizen in the United States

In the United States, the government gets its power to govern from the people. We have a government of the people, by the people, and for the people. Citizens in the United States shape their government and its policies, so they must learn about important public issues and get involved in their communities. Citizens vote in free elections to choose important government officials, such as the President, Vice President, Senators, and Representatives. All citizens can call their elected officials to express an opinion, ask for information, or get help with specific issues.

Our government is based on several important values: freedom, opportunity, equality, and justice. Americans share these values, and these values give us a common civic identity.

Government in the United States protects the rights of each person. The United States is made up of people from different backgrounds, cultures, and religions. Our government and laws are organized so that citizens from different backgrounds and with different beliefs all have the same rights. No one can be punished or harmed for having an opinion or belief that is different from that of most other people.

OF, BY, AND FOR THE PEOPLE: WHAT IS DEMOCRACY?

The word "democracy" means "government by the people." Democracy can have different forms in different countries. In the United States, we have what is called "representative democracy." This means that the people choose officials to represent their views and concerns in government.

How the United States Began

The early colonists and settlers who came to the United States were often fleeing unfair treatment, especially religious persecution, in their home countries. They were seeking freedom and new opportunities. Today, many people come to the United States for these same reasons.

Before it became a separate and independent nation, the United States was made up of 13 colonies that were ruled by Great Britain. People living in the colonies had no say in which laws were passed or how they were governed. They especially objected to "taxation without representation." This means that people had to pay taxes, but they had no say in how their government operated.

By 1776, many people felt that this was unfair and that they should govern themselves. Representatives from the colonies issued a Declaration of Independence. This important document declared that the colonies were free and independent and no longer tied to Great Britain. Thomas Jefferson wrote the Declaration of Independence. He later became the third president of the United States.

WHAT YOU CAN DO

As a permanent resident, you have many rights and freedoms. In return, you have some responsibilities. One important responsibility is to get involved in your community. You should also learn about the American way of life and our history and government. You can do this by taking adult education classes and reading the local newspaper.

THE UNITED STATES AND THE ORIGINAL THIRTEEN COLONIES

The thirteen colonies were founded in the following order: Virginia, Massachusetts, Maryland, Connecticut, Rhode Island, Delaware, New Hampshire, North Carolina, South Carolina, New Jersey, New York, Pennsylvania, and Georgia.

The Declaration of Independence was signed on July 4, 1776. This is the reason that Americans celebrate July 4th every year as Independence Day: it is our nation's birthday.

The United States had to fight for its freedom from Great Britain in the Revolutionary War. General George Washington led the military forces of the American Revolution. He is known as the "Father of Our Country." Later he became the first president of the United States.

After the colonies won the war, they became states. Each state had its own government. The people in these states wanted to create a new form of government to unite the states into a single nation. Today, this central government, our national government, is called "the federal government." The United States now consists of 50 states, the District of Columbia (a special area that is the home of the federal government), the territories of Guam, American Samoa, and the U.S. Virgin Islands, and the commonwealths of the Northern Mariana Islands and Puerto Rico.

"ALL MEN ARE CREATED EQUAL"

Many Americans know these words from the Declaration of Independence by heart:

"We hold these truths to be self-evident, that all men are created equal, that they are endowed by their Creator with certain unalienable Rights, that among these are Life, Liberty and the pursuit of Happiness."

This means that all people are born with the same basic rights. Government does not create these rights, and no government can take these rights away.

Creating "A More Perfect Union"

For several years after the American Revolution, the states tried different ways to join together in a central government, but this government was too weak. So representatives from each of the states gathered in Philadelphia, Pennsylvania in 1787 to develop a new, stronger central government. This meeting was the Constitutional Convention. After much debate, leaders from the states drafted a document describing this new government. This document is the U.S. Constitution, one of the most important documents in American history. The Constitution described how the new government would be organized, how government officials would be chosen, and what rights the new central government would guarantee to citizens.

The members of the Constitutional Convention approved the Constitution on September 17, 1787. Next, all 13 states had to approve it. Some people felt

"OLD GLORY"—THE UNITED STATES FLAG

The United States flag has changed over our history. Now it has 13 stripes to represent the original 13 American colonies. It has 50 stars, one for each state. The American national anthem was written about the flag and is called "The Star-Spangled Banner." The flag is also called the "Stars and Stripes," and a favorite American song is called "Stars and Stripes Forever."

that the Constitution did not do enough to protect the rights of individual people. The states agreed to approve the Constitution if a list of individual rights were added to it. The states approved the Constitution in 1789. This list of individual rights, called the Bill of Rights, was added to the Constitution in 1791. Changes to the Constitution are called "amendments." The first 10 amendments to the Constitution are called the Bill of Rights.

The United States is a nation governed by laws. Government officials make decisions based on those laws. The Constitution is known as the "supreme law of the land" because every citizen, including all government officials, and every law that is created must uphold the principles of the Constitution. Laws apply equally to everyone. The federal government has limited powers. Powers not given directly to the federal government by the Constitution are held by the states.

"WE THE PEOPLE"

"We the People" are the first three words of the U.S. Constitution. The Constitution begins by explaining why it was written and what it was intended to accomplish. This section is called the "preamble." Here is the preamble to the Constitution:

"We the People of the United States, in Order to form a more perfect Union, establish Justice, insure domestic Tranquility, provide for the common defense, promote the general Welfare, and secure the Blessings of Liberty to ourselves and our Posterity, do ordain and establish this Constitution for the United States of America."

The Bill of Rights: The First 10 Amendments

The first changes to the Constitution were made to protect individual citizens and to limit the power of government. The Bill of Rights lists important freedoms that are promised to the American people. In most instances, these rights limit what government can do to individual people. These rights include:

- Freedom of speech. The government cannot tell people what to say or not say. People can say what they want about public issues without fear of punishment.

- Freedom of religion. The government cannot tell people what place of worship to attend. People can choose to worship—or not worship—as they please.

- Freedom of the press. The government cannot decide what is printed in newspapers or heard on radio and TV.

- Freedom to gather in public places. The government cannot stop people from holding lawful public gatherings for many different purposes.

CHANGING THE CONSTITUTION

The U.S. Constitution is called a "living document" because the American people, acting through their state and national representatives, can change it when necessary. These changes are called "amendments." It is a long and difficult process to change the Constitution, so it has been changed only 27 times over the course of our history. Besides the Bill of Rights, some important amendments are the Thirteenth, which forbids slavery, and the Fourteenth, which guarantees all citizens equal protection under the law. The Nineteenth Amendment gives women the right to vote.

- Freedom to own firearms. The government cannot prevent people from owning guns.

- Freedom to protest government actions and demand change. The government cannot silence or punish people who challenge government actions they don't agree with.

The Bill of Rights also guarantees "due process." Due process is a set of specific legal procedures that must be followed when someone is accused of a crime. Police officers and soldiers cannot stop and search a person without good reason, and they cannot search people's homes without permission from a court. Persons accused of a crime are guaranteed a speedy trial by a jury made up of people like themselves. They are guaranteed legal representation and can call witnesses to speak for them. Cruel and unusual punishment is also forbidden.

How the Federal Government Works

The original 13 colonies had lived under the total power of the British king. In their new central government, Americans wanted to prevent a concentration of power in one government official or one office. The Constitution created three branches for the federal government, so that power would be balanced. The three branches have separate responsibilities. We call this the system of "checks and balances." No single branch of government can become too powerful because it is balanced by the other two branches.

THE FEDERAL GOVERNMENT

The three branches of the federal government are:

The Legislative branch:
the U.S. Congress and
related offices

The Executive branch:
the President, Vice President, and
departments of the federal government

The Judicial branch:
the Supreme Court of the United States
and federal courts across the country

The Legislative Branch: Congress

Citizens of the United States vote in free elections to choose people to represent them in the U.S. Congress. Congress has the responsibility of making the laws for our nation. Congress is made up of the House of Representatives and the Senate.

The U.S. House of Representatives

People in each state vote to choose members of the House of Representatives. There are 435 members of the House of Representatives, which is often called "the House." The number of representatives from each state depends on how many people live in that state. States are divided into districts. People living in each district vote for someone to represent their district in the House. Each representative serves for two years, and then people have another chance to vote for them or for a different person to represent them. Representatives can serve in Congress for an unlimited period of time.

There are five additional members in the House. These are the representatives of the District of Columbia and the territories of Puerto Rico, Guam, American Samoa, and the U.S. Virgin Islands. They may participate in debates,

GOVERNMENT OFFICIALS SERVE THE PEOPLE

In the United States, everyone can call their elected Representative and Senators. You can call 202-224-3121 and ask for your Representative's or Senators' offices. You can write to your Representative or Senators to ask questions or give your opinion about legislation and the federal government, or if you have a problem and need help with federal benefits.

To write to your Representative:
The Honorable (add Representative's full name)
U.S. House of Representatives
Washington, DC 20515

To write to your Senator:
The Honorable (add Senator's full name)
United States Senate
Washington, DC 20510

You can visit the websites of Congress to learn about current activities in the House and Senate and about your own Representative and Senators, including their website addresses.

- For the House of Representatives, visit http://www.house.gov/.

- For the Senate, visit http://www.senate.gov/.

but they cannot participate in the formal votes of the entire House.

The House of Representatives makes laws, but it has some special responsibilities. Only the House of Representatives can:

- Propose laws about taxes.

- Decide if a government official accused of committing a crime against the country should be put on trial in the Senate. This is called "impeachment."

The U.S. Senate

There are 100 Senators in the U.S. Senate. People in each state vote to choose two Senators to represent them in Congress. Senators serve for six years, and then people have another chance to vote for them or for a different person to represent them. Senators can serve in Congress for an unlimited period of time. Senators make laws, but they also have special responsibilities.

WHAT YOU CAN DO

Learn about your Representative and Senators and what they are doing to represent you in Congress. You can do this by looking for stories about them in your local newspaper and visiting the websites for Congress. All Senators and Representatives have local offices in their home communities; you can find these listed in the blue pages of the phone book. If you visit Washington, DC, you can take a free tour of the U.S. Capitol, where Congress works.

You can learn about the President by visiting the website for the White House, the President's home. Visit http://www.whitehouse.gov/ .

Only the Senate can:

- Say "yes" or "no" to any agreements the President makes with other countries or organizations of countries. These are called "treaties."

- Say "yes" or "no" to any person the President chooses for high-level jobs, such as Supreme Court judges or officials to run the federal departments, such as the Department of Education or the Department of Health and Human Services.

- Hold a trial for a government official who commits a crime against the United States.

The Executive Branch: The President

The President is the leader of the executive branch and is responsible for upholding and enforcing the laws of the country. The President has many other responsibilities, too, such as setting national policies, proposing laws to Congress, and choosing high-level officials and members of the Supreme Court. The President also is the leader of the U.S. military and may be called the Commander-in-Chief.

People vote in elections for the President and Vice President every four years. The President can only serve in office for 2 four-year terms. The Vice President becomes President if the President becomes disabled or dies.

The Judicial Branch:
The Supreme Court

The Constitution created the Supreme Court, the highest court in the United States. There are nine judges on the Supreme Court. They are called "justices." The President chooses the members of the Supreme Court, and they serve as long as they are able. The Supreme Court can overrule both state and federal laws if they conflict with the Constitution. There are other federal courts, such as the U.S. District Courts and the U.S. Circuit Courts of Appeals.

To learn more about the U.S. Supreme Court, visit http://www.supremecourtus.gov.

State and Local Government

In addition to the federal government, each state has its own constitution and its own government. Each state government also has three branches: legislative, executive, and judicial.

The leader of the state executive branch is called the "governor." The people of each state vote in elections to choose their governor and their representatives to the state legislature. The state legislature makes the laws that

apply in each state. These laws cannot conflict with the U.S. Constitution, and each state judicial branch upholds the laws of that state.

Each state also has local governments. There are city or county governments or sometimes both. They provide and oversee many serv-ices in your local community, such as public schools and libraries, police and fire departments, and water, gas, and electric services. People in local communities usually vote for local government officials, but some local officials are appointed. Local governments have different forms. Some have mayors as their leaders; some have city councils or county councils. Local communities also have school boards, citizens who are elected or appointed to oversee the public schools.

WHAT YOU CAN DO

Many local government meetings are open to the public. Many are held at night so that anyone can attend. For example, you can go to a city council meeting or a school board meeting to learn more about what is going on in your community. These meetings and their times and locations are usually listed in the local newspaper. The meetings may be listed on the local government's website. Some local government meetings also are on television on local cable stations.

Becoming a U.S. Citizen

Becoming a U.S. citizen gives permanent residents new rights and privileges. Citizenship also brings with it new responsibilities. This section offers some reasons to consider becoming a U.S. citizen and describes what you need to do to become a citizen.

To become a citizen, you must be willing to swear your loyalty to the United States. You must give up your allegiance to any other country. You must agree to support and defend the U.S. Constitution. When you become a citizen, you accept all of the responsibilities of being an American. In return, you get certain rights and privileges of citizenship.

Why Become a U.S. Citizen?

Permanent residents have most of the rights of U.S. citizens. But there are many important reasons to consider becoming a U.S. citizen. Here are some good reasons:

- **Showing your patriotism.** Becoming a citizen is a way to demonstrate your commitment to your new country.

- **Voting.** Only citizens can vote in federal elections.

- **Serving on a jury.** Only U.S. citizens can serve on a jury. Serving on a jury is an important responsibility for U.S. citizens.

- **Traveling with a U.S. passport.** A U.S. passport enables you to get assistance from the U.S. government when overseas, if necessary.

- **Bringing family members to the U.S.** U.S. citizens generally get priority when petitioning to bring family members permanently to this country.

- **Obtaining citizenship for children born abroad.** In most cases, a child born abroad to a U.S. citizen is automatically a U.S. citizen.

- **Becoming eligible for federal jobs.** Certain jobs with government agencies require U.S. citizenship.

- **Becoming an elected official.** Many elected offices in this country require U.S. citizenship.

- **Meeting tax requirements.** Tax requirements may be different for U.S. citizens and permanent residents.

- **Keeping your residency.** A U.S. citizen's right to remain in the United States cannot be taken away.

- **Becoming eligible for federal grants and scholarships.** Many financial aid grants, including college scholarships and funds given by the government for specific purposes, are available only to U.S. citizens.

- **Obtaining government benefits.** Some government benefits are available only to U.S. citizens.

Naturalization: Becoming a Citizen

The process of becoming a U.S. citizen is called "naturalization." You can apply for naturalization once you meet the following requirements:

Live in the U.S. for at least 5 years as a permanent resident (or 3 years if married to and living with a U.S. citizen).

Be present in the U.S. for at least 30 months out of the past 5 years (or 18 months out of the past 3 years if married to and living with a U.S. citizen).

Live within a state or district for at least 3 months before you apply.

You may have to follow different rules if:

- You, or your deceased parent, spouse, or child, have served in the U.S. Armed Forces.

- You are a U.S. national.

- You obtained permanent residence through the 1986 amnesty law.

- You are a refugee or asylee.

- You have a U.S. citizen spouse who is regularly stationed abroad.

- You lost U.S. citizenship under prior law because of marriage to a non-citizen.

- You are an employee of certain types of companies or nonprofit organizations.

GETTING NATURALIZATION INFORMATION

People 18 years or older who want to become citizens should get Form M-476, *A Guide to Naturalization*. This guide has important information on the requirements for naturalization. It also describes the forms you will need to begin the naturalization process.

To see if you are eligible to apply for naturalization, see Form M-480, Naturalization Eligibility Worksheet, at the end of *A Guide to Naturalization*. Use Form N-400 to apply for naturalization. There is a fee to file Form N-400.

To get Forms M-476, M-480, and N-400, call the USCIS Forms Line at 1-800-870-3676 or get them from http://www.uscis.gov.

Consult *A Guide to Naturalization* for more information. You may also wish to consult an immigration attorney or other qualified professional.

Requirements for Naturalization

The general requirements for naturalization are:

1. Live in the U.S. as a permanent resident for a specific amount of time (Continuous Residence).

2. Be present in the U.S. for specific time periods (Physical Presence).

3. Spend specific amounts of time in your state or district (Time in District or State).

4. Behave in a legal and acceptable manner (Good Moral Character).

5. Know English and information about U.S. history and government (English and Civics).

6. Understand and accept the principles of the U.S. Constitution (Attachment to the Constitution).

MAINTAINING CONTINUOUS RESIDENCE (CR) AS A PERMANENT RESIDENT

If you leave the U.S. for:	Your CR status is:	To keep your status you must:
More than 6 months	Possibly broken	Prove that you continued to live, work, and/or have ties to the U.S. (e.g., paid taxes) while you were away.
More than 1 year	Broken	In most cases, you must begin your continuous residence over. Apply for a re-entry permit before you leave if you plan to return to the U.S. as a permanent resident.

1. Continuous Residence

"Continuous residence" means that you must live in the U.S. as a permanent resident for a certain period of time. Most people must be permanent residents in continuous residence for 5 years (or 3 years if married to a U.S. citizen) before they can begin the naturalization process. For refugees, this means 5 years from the date you arrived in the U.S., which is usually the date you obtained permanent resident status. For those granted asylum status in the U.S., this period begins 1 year before you got permanent resident status. The date on your Permanent Resident Card is the date your 5 years begins. If you leave the United States for a long period of time, usually 6 months or more, you may "break" your continuous residence.

PRESERVING YOUR RESIDENCE FOR NATURALIZATION PURPOSES: EXEMPTIONS FOR 1-YEAR ABSENCES

If you work for the U.S. government, a recognized U.S. research institution, or certain U.S. corporations, or if you are a member of the clergy serving abroad, you may be able to preserve your continuous residence if you:

1. Have been physically present and living in the U.S. without leaving for at least one year after becoming a permanent resident.

2. Submit Form N-470, Application to Preserve Residence for Naturalization Purposes, before you have been outside the U.S. for one year. There is a fee to file Form N-470.

For more information, contact the USCIS Forms Line at: 1-800-870-3676 and ask for Form N-470, Application to Preserve Residence for Naturalization Purposes. You can also get the form on the USCIS website at http://uscis.gov/graphics/formsfee/forms/n-470.htm .

If you leave the United States for 1 year or longer, you may be able to return if you have a re-entry permit. You should apply for this re-entry permit before you depart the United States. See page 10 for information on how to apply for a re-entry permit. In most cases, none of the time you were in the United States before you left the country will count toward your time in continuous residence. This means that you will need to begin your continuous residence again after you return to the United States, and you may have to wait up to 4 years and 1 day before you can apply for naturalization.

TIP: A re-entry permit (Form I-131) and the Application to Preserve Residence for Naturalization Purposes (Form N-470) are not the same. A re-entry permit lets you re-enter the U.S. as a permanent resident if you have been outside of the U.S. for more than 12 months. Form N-470 lets certain people maintain their continuous residence for naturalization purposes if they will be outside the U.S. for more than 12 months.

EXEMPTIONS FOR MILITARY PERSONNEL

If you are on active-duty status or were recently discharged from the U.S. Armed Forces, the continuous residence and physical presence requirements may not apply to you. You can find more information in the M-599 Naturalization Information for Military Personnel brochure. Every military base should have a point-of-contact to handle your naturalization application and certify a Form N-426, Request for Certification of Military or Naval Service. You must submit Form N-426 with your application forms. To get the forms you need, call the USCIS Forms Line at: 1-800-870-3676 and ask for the Military Packet. You can find the M-599 and Form N-426 at http://www.uscis.gov.

Be aware that absences from the United States while your naturalization application is pending could cause problems with your eligibility, especially if you accept employment abroad.

2. Physical Presence in the United States

"Physical presence" means that you actually have been  present in the United States. If you are a permanent resident at least 18 years old, you must be physically present in the United States for at least 30 months during the last 5 years (or 18 months during the last 3 years, if married to a U.S. citizen) before you apply for naturalization.

"PHYSICAL PRESENCE"

Q: What is the difference between "physical presence" and "continuous residence"?

A: "Physical presence" is the total days you were inside the United States and does not include the time you spend outside the U.S. Each day you spend outside the U.S. takes away from your "physical presence" total. If you are away from the U.S. for long periods of time or if you take many short trips outside the U.S., you may not meet your "physical presence" requirement. To count your "physical presence" time, you should add together all the time you have been in the United States. Then subtract all trips you have taken outside the United States. This includes short trips to Canada and Mexico. For example, if you go to Mexico for a weekend, you must include the trip when counting how many days you spent out of the country.

"Continuous residence" is the total time you have resided as a permanent resident in the United States before applying for naturalization. If you spend too much time outside the United States during a single trip, you may break your "continuous residence."

3. Time as a Resident in District or State

Most people must live in the district or state where they apply for naturalization for at least 3 months. Students can apply for naturalization either where they go to school or where their family lives (if they depend on their parents for support).

4. Good Moral Character

To be eligible for naturalization, you must be a person of good moral character. A person is not considered to be of "good moral character" if they commit certain crimes during the 5 years before they apply for naturalization or if they lie during their naturalization interview.

BEHAVIORS THAT MIGHT SHOW A LACK OF GOOD MORAL CHARACTER

- Drunk driving or being drunk most of the time.
- Illegal gambling.
- Prostitution.
- Lying to gain immigration benefits.
- Failing to pay court-ordered child support.
- Committing terrorist acts.
- Persecuting someone because of race, religion, national origin, political opinion, or social group.

If you commit some specific crimes, you can never become a U.S. citizen and will probably be removed from the country. These crimes are called "bars" to naturalization. Crimes called "aggravated felonies" (if committed on or after November 29, 1990), including: murder, rape, sexual abuse of a child, violent assault, treason, and trafficking in drugs, firearms, or people are some examples of permanent bars to naturalization. In most cases, immigrants who were exempted or discharged from serving in the U.S. Armed Forces because they were immigrants and immigrants who deserted from the U.S. Armed Forces are also permanently barred from U.S. citizenship.

You also may be denied citizenship if you behave in other ways that show you lack good moral character.

Other crimes are temporary bars to naturalization. Temporary bars usually prevent you from becoming a citizen for up to 5 years after you commit the crime. These include:

- Any crime against a person with intent to harm.

- Any crime against property or the government involving fraud.

- 2 or more crimes with combined sentences of 5 years or more.

- Violating controlled substance laws (e.g., using or selling illegal drugs).

- Spending 180 days or more during the past 5 years in jail or prison.

Report any crimes that you committed when you apply for naturalization. This includes crimes removed from your record or committed before your 18th birthday. If you do not tell USCIS about them, you may be denied citizenship and you could be prosecuted.

5. English and Civics

In general, you must show that you can read, write, and speak basic English. You also must have a basic knowledge of U.S. history and government (also known as "civics"). You will be required to pass a test of English and a test of civics to prove your knowledge.

Many schools and community organizations help people prepare for their citizenship tests. You can find examples of test questions in *A Guide to Naturalization*. You can get materials to help you study for these tests and practice tests on the USCIS website at http://uscis.gov/graphics/services/natz/require.htm.

6. Attachment to the Constitution

You must be willing to support and defend the United States and its Constitution. You declare your "attachment" or loyalty to the United States and the Constitution

EXEMPTIONS TO THE ENGLISH AND CIVICS REQUIREMENTS

Some people who apply for naturalization have different test requirements because of their age and the length of time they have lived in the U.S.

If you are	Lived as permanent resident in the U.S. for	You do not take the	You must take the
Over age 50	20 years	English test	civics test in your language
Over age 55	15 years	English test	civics test in your language
Over age 65	20 years	English test	simplified civics test in your language

If you do not have to take the English test, you must bring your own translator for the civics test. If you have a physical or mental disability, you may not have to take either test if you file Form N-648, Medical Certification for Disability Exceptions, with your application. To get more information, contact the USCIS Forms Line at 1-800-870-3676 and ask for Form N-648 or get a copy from the USCIS website at http://www.uscis.gov/graphics/formsfee/forms/n-648.html.

when you take the Oath of Allegiance. You become a U.S. citizen when you take the Oath of Allegiance.

People who show they have a physical or developmental disability that makes them unable to understand the meaning of the oath do not have to take the Oath of Allegiance.

If you have a pending naturalization application and you move, you must notify USCIS of your new address. You can call 1-800-375-5283 to report your new address. You must also file Form AR-11 with DHS. See page 12 for instructions.

Naturalization Ceremonies

 If USCIS approves your application for naturalization, you must attend a ceremony and take the Oath of Allegiance. USCIS will send you a Form N-445, Notice of Naturalization Oath Ceremony, to tell you the time and date of your ceremony. You must complete this form and bring it to your ceremony.

If you cannot go to your ceremony, you can reschedule your ceremony. To reschedule, you must return Form N-445 to your local USCIS office along with a letter explaining why you cannot attend the ceremony.

You will return your Permanent Resident Card to USCIS when you check in at the Oath ceremony. You will no longer need your card because you will get a Certificate of Naturalization at the ceremony.

You are not a citizen until you have taken the Oath of Allegiance. An official will read each part of the Oath slowly and ask you to repeat the words. After you take the Oath, you will receive your Certificate of Naturalization. This certificate proves that you are a U.S. citizen.

The Oath of Allegiance ceremony is a public event. Many communities hold special ceremonies on Independence Day, July 4th, of each year. Check to see if your community holds a special July 4th citizenship ceremony and how you can participate. Many people bring their families and celebrate after the ceremony.

THE UNITED STATES TODAY*

*The United States also includes the territories of Guam, American Samoa, and the U.S. Virgin Islands, and the commonwealths of the Northern Mariana Islands and Puerto Rico, which do not appear on this map.

FEDERAL HOLIDAYS

The federal government observes the following official holidays. Most federal offices are closed on these days. If a holiday falls on a Saturday, it is observed on the preceding Friday. If a holiday falls on a Sunday, it is observed on the following Monday. Many employers also give their employees a holiday on these days.

New Year's Day	January 1st
Birthday of Martin Luther King, Jr.	3rd Monday in January
Presidents' Day	3rd Monday in February
Memorial Day	Last Monday in May
Independence Day	July 4th
Labor Day	1st Monday in September
Columbus Day	2nd Monday in October
Veterans Day	November 11th
Thanksgiving Day	4th Thursday in November
Christmas Day	December 25th

ADDITIONAL INFORMATION FOR THIS GUIDE

Page 11, right photograph courtesy of http://www.goarmy.com.

Page 40, text box, top photograph by Gerald L. Nino.

Page 85, top right, Oval Office photograph by Paul Morse.

Pages 1, 14, 29, 66, 68, and 70 (left column), photographs by John Vavricka.